Self-Management

A GUIDE FOR THE SMALL COMMUNITY ASSOCIATION

2nd Edition

Debra H. Lewin
Ellen Hirsch de Haan, Esq.
Editors

Community Associations Press
Alexandria, VA

ISBN: 0-944715-66-4

Self-Management: A Guide for the Small Community Association, 2nd Edition
© 2001 Community Associations Press, a Division of Community Associations Institute.
No part of this publication may be reproduced in whole or in part without the express,
written consent of the publisher. Please direct inquiries to CAI, 225 Reinekers Lane, Suite
300, Alexandria, VA 22314.

To order additional copies of this product, please write to the publisher at the address
below or call (703) 548-8600. You can also order online at www.caionline.org.

*This publication is designed to provide accurate and authoritative information in regard to the subject matter
covered. It is sold with the understanding that the publisher is not engaged in rendering legal, accounting, or
other professional services. If legal advice or other expert assistance is required, the services of a competent professional should be sought.*
　　　–From a Declaration of Principles, jointly adopted by a Committee of the American
　　　　Bar Association and a Committee of Publishers.

Library of Congress Cataloging-in-Publication Data
Self-management: a guide for the small community association / Debra H. Lewin, editor.—
2nd ed.
　　　p. cm
　　ISBN 0-944715-66-4 (pbk.)
　　1. Homeowners' associations—United States-Management. 2. Condominium associa-
　　tions-United States—Management. 3. Housing management—United States. I.
　　Lewin, Debra H., 1948— II. Community Associations Institute.

　　HD7287.82.U6 S45 2001
　　643'.2-dc21

　　　　　　　　　　　　　　　　　　　　　　　　　　　　　　　　　2001053686

Community Associations Press
A Division of Community Associations Institute
225 Reinekers Lane, Suite 300
Alexandria, VA 22314

Printed in the United States of America

Contents

Part II: Areas of Operation

Acknowledgments

Editors
Debra H. Lewin
Ellen Hirsch de Haan, Esq.

Reviewers
Richard S. Ekimoto, Esq., Honolulu, HI
Loura Sanchez, Esq., Wheat Ridge, CO
Clifford J. Treese, CPCU, ARM, Honolulu, HI
Molly Foley-Healy, JD
Kris Cook, CAE

CAI President
Barbara Byrd Keenan, CAE

Contributors to the First Edition

David E. Cane, Esq.
Rodney D. Clark
Ellen Hirsch de Haan, Esq.
Christopher Durso
Kenneth Egbert, AMS, PCAM
Seth Emmer, Esq.
Mitchell H. Frumkin, P.E., P.P., RS
Edward Guttenplan, CPA
Dave Hocksprung, CPA
Mary M. Howell, Esq.

Marc D. Markel, Esq.
James J. McDonald, Jr., Esq.
Robert Nordlund, P.E., RS
J.A.G. "Buddy" Parrish
Julia Pheifer
Brett Pselly
Keith Soares
Debbie Taras-Paquariello, CIC, CPIW
Barbara D. Wick, CPCU, ARM, AIS
Debora M. Zumwalt, Esq.

Introduction to the Second Edition

Community associations are unique entities—part corporate business, part government municipality, part community. Governing and managing these hybrids is no small challenge—even in the smallest of associations. Most community associations assign the policy setting to an elected board and assign the management of day-to-day operations to a professional manager. For a few associations, however, these differing functions are combined in one extraordinary group of dedicated people—the self-managing board. These are highly committed individuals who make countless sacrifices on behalf of their communities, and it was for them that *Self-Management: A Guide for the Small Association* was first written.

Whether you're self managing a condominium, cooperative, homeowner association, or other mandatory-membership community association, this guide is intended to help you fill the dual roles of governance and management without the benefit of professional management services.

The second edition of *Self-Management* has been significantly expanded to include additional information on nearly every topic covered in the first edition. Nevertheless, it is, as the name states, a guide. It doesn't attempt to be a comprehensive treatise on all aspects of a self manager's responsibility, but it does contain enough basic information to get you started in the right direction. If this guide makes you aware of the nature and scope of your responsibility, if it helps you avoid problems, if it makes your job just a little less formidable, it will have accomplished its purpose.

As in so many endeavors, education will be a key ingredient in your success as a self manager. Reading this book is a good first step. At the end of each chapter you'll find information about related resources that will continue your education. Many of the recommended resources are GAP Reports—Guides for Association Practitioners. That's what self managers are—association practitioners. As this second edition of *Self-Management* goes to press, there are 28 titles in the GAP series, and more are planned for the future. Possibly one of the best and most comprehensive guides to self managing an association would be a complete set of these reports.

Community Associations Institute (CAI) also provides other educational resources for those who are self managing their community associations, and you'll find more information about CAI at the end this book.

The principles and information contained in *Self-Management* are relevant to all community associations regardless of their size. Some small associations employ professional management services and some large associations function very successfully with volunteer managers. Regardless of your situation, this guide will be extremely useful.

Numerous experts in all areas of community association management contributed their expertise to the content of this guide. It represents the combined wisdom of managers, accountants, attorneys, reserve specialists, engineers, insurance specialists, and parliamentarians—all of whom are recognized leaders in the community associations industry. Their shared expertise will make your job a little easier and your experiences more enjoyable.

Part I: Areas of Responsibility

Chapter 1

An Overview
of Community Associations

When developers first started building community associations, everyone agreed that having property shared by all owners was a good idea. Deciding who would take care of it led to the idea of an association of owners. And so, community associations were created to maintain, repair, and replace common property; ensure compliance with laws, codes, rules, and ordinances; enforce the covenants and restrictions in the governing documents; and maintain the property value.

Community associations are governed by a board of directors, elected by the members to handle the responsibilities of the association. Their actions and responsibilities are set forth in association governing documents and certain state and federal laws. Boards have legal responsibilities—as well as liabilities—even though they are volunteers.

The Evolution of Community Associations

Rudimentary planned communities were built as early as 1831, although they did not become an established form of housing until the turn of the century. At that time, America was struggling to control both urban growth and suburbanization by emphasizing carefully designed development practices that were supported by municipal laws and private covenants. Planned communities were the natural outgrowth of this struggle.

Cooperative housing developed in response to the housing shortage that occurred following World War I and World War II. Cooperative housing was originally established to provide quality low- and moderate-income housing. Although some cooperatives still provide moderately priced housing, today others provide housing for the most affluent segments of society.

Condominium developments were established to satisfy the significant housing demand fueled by an expanding economy in the late 1960s and early 1970s. The nation's first condominium, The Greystoke, was built in Salt Lake City, Utah in 1962.

Today, with the increasing scarcity of land in large metropolitan areas and the high cost of housing, the number and popularity of community associations continues to increase. Consider, for example, that in 1990, nearly one out of every eight Americans (32 million) lived in a community association.

In 1990, there were nearly five million condominium units, 824,000 cooperative units, and almost six million planned-community units. In 1993, there were an estimated 150,000 community associations, with 40,000 existing in Florida and 25,000 in California, and every other state, including Alaska and Hawaii. If associations have an average of five board members, California needed 125,000 and Florida needed 200,000 board members just to operate the community associations existing in those states in 1993.

In 1993, between 50 and 75 percent of all new home sales in the largest metropolitan areas were for homes in common-interest communities.

Types of Community Associations

There are five basic types of community associations.

Planned communities are those in which individuals own their lots or houses separate from their neighbors, but membership in the association is nevertheless mandatory. The association owns the common area, but the owners have very specific rights and obligations with respect to the common area. In California, the common area also may be owned in common by the lot owners, but this is the exception. In all other states, the association owns the common area.

In a planned community, common areas may include grounds, recreational areas, drainage ponds, and sometimes, roads. However, they don't generally include walls and roofs because most planned communities consist of detached housing.

Cooperatives are properties owned by a corporation in which individuals own a shared interest and the exclusive right to occupy a specific portion of the property—usually an apartment. Because most cooperatives comprise a building, the common area in a cooperative often consists of hallways, elevators, roofs, parking areas, and laundry facilities.

Another type of cooperative is the California Community Apartment Project, in which title to all the units is held by all owners as tenants in common, and each owner has an occupancy agreement for exclusive use of his or her own unit.

Yet another type of cooperative is the Real Estate Cooperative, in which the unit and membership interest in the association are "real estate for all purposes" and not personal property as is typically the case.

Condominiums are associations where an individual owns a separate unit or apartment and shares ownership of the common area with all the other owners. If the condominium community has attached units, the common areas may

Characteristics of Mandatory-Membership Community Associations

1. Owners are automatically members of the association.

2. Owners are bound to the association on a mutual basis by the governing documents that are covenants that "run with the land."

3. Owners are assessed fees to cover the costs of operating the association and the community. Owners who fail to pay are subject to legal action by the association including liens and foreclosure.

4. Owners share a property interest in the common areas and the whole community.

be similar to those in a cooperative. If the condominiums are detached, the common areas may be similar to those in a planned community.

A condominium differs from the other common-interest communities because owners generally co-own the common areas. How much of the common area each person owns can vary. It can be a simple fraction (each of 100 owners owns 1/100 of the common area) or it can be a ratio that depends on the size of an owner's unit. As long as some common area is co-owned by individuals, the association also may own property, such as a parking lot or clubhouse facility, as it does in a cooperative and planned community, depending on state law.

Community apartment projects are those in which people own the building or other property that makes up the community, and each person owns the right to occupy a unit. This community is similar to a cooperative because people own the exclusive right to occupy a unit. But, unlike a cooperative, owners (not a corporation) own the property as tenants in common. This type of common-interest community only exists in California.

Master associations are combinations of the various forms of community associations listed above. The master community association serves as an umbrella association. For example, a master community can consist of two condominium buildings and a planned community. A person who owns a unit in one of these condominiums has an individual interest in his or her unit, a fractional shared interest in the condominium common area, and a shared interest with all the members of the master association in the master association common area.

The terms above describe the type of ownership, not a type of building. but sometimes common-interest communities are described as garden apartments, patio apartments, and town homes. These aren't legal terms; they're architectural or marketing terms. Whether a town home is a condominium or planned community depends on who owns the common area. It's a condominium if the common areas belong to the unit owners as tenants-in-common. If not, it's probably a planned community.

Mixed-Use Associations

Another development in the evolution of community associations is mixed-use associations, in which the community association governs both residential and commercial uses. Like a master association, a mixed-use association can be made up of sub-associations—individual condominium, cooperative, and planned community associations. These sub-associations are separate community associations in their own right with their own governing documents and structure; and they can be any number and combination of condominium associations, cooperative associations, or planned community associations. Each of the individual sub-associations, however, must belong to the master association.

Master associations differ from mixed-use associations in that they're almost always purely residential, and each of the sub-associations is a residential housing association. A mixed-use association is almost always a mixture of residential sub-associations and commercial and/or industrial (i.e., non-residential) sub-associations.

Something for Everyone

Community associations can be found in a variety of architectural types: single family detached houses, townhouses, duplexes, quadraplexes, two- and three-story garden-style, mid- and high-rise buildings. Manufactured housing communities may be condominiums. Condominiums and cooperatives are found with any architectural type; but, generally, they are the only form that can be used where units are stacked, as in low-, mid-, or high-rise developments. There are also many types of non-residential condominium association properties such as office buildings, medical suites, docks, and parking garages.

Buyers generally choose to live in a community association for three primary reasons: protection and enhancement of property values, services and amenities, and affordability. The community association lifestyle attracts all kinds of residents—depending on their age, income, career, and family status. In general, the low-maintenance, amenities, security, and affordability appeal to just about everyone at some time in their lives.

Empty nesters—people without children or whose children have grown up and moved out—are especially attracted by the low maintenance, amenities, and security of community association living.

Community associations offer affordable homeownership for those with a single or limited income—whether singles, families, or retirees. However, many double-income families—who can afford traditional homes—prefer community association living because they don't have to spend time on maintenance. Also, many first-time buyers find it easier to enter the real estate market with the relatively lower cost of coop, condominium, and planned community units. And, of course, community associations appeal to investors because they often compensate for shortages in the local rental markets.

Overall, community associations offer a broad spectrum of lifestyle choices for many people in today's society.

Taking Over From the Developer

As a self-managing board of a small association, it's likely you live in a new association, and you're working with a developer to gradually assume control of that association. You're at an important phase of your community's evolution, so a smooth and efficient transition is important.

The developer chartered the association early in the planning process, and long before the first home was sold. But, as sales begin, a shared interest emerges. Because the developer has a substantial investment in the association, he or she will be motivated to work with you and contribute to your success. It's not only good business practice, but it's also very likely legally required by the state.

By creating common property, developers can offer prospective buyers more perks for their money. Also, developers who retain some interest in the property after homes are sold protect their investment by having a board of directors to oversee the property. Once the developer has moved on, the association serves residents as a private, nonprofit organization to oversee shared property.

Developers usually own units, lots, or apartments in the community before they transfer control to residents or owners. The more smoothly the association operates before it is transferred to the owners the better protected the developer's investment will be.

Governing documents and state law usually dictate when control should transfer from the developer to the owners. Some states require that the owners gain control when 75 percent of the units have been sold; some require transfer within a specific period of time after the initial sale.

At this point, the association, in turn, protects the shared interests that exist in planned communities, condominiums, and cooperatives. It provides an organized and productive business operation, governance, communication, rules notification and enforcement, and fosters a sense of community to help enhance residents' enjoyment of their homes.

During the transition, the best thing you can do is communicate openly and frequently with the developer. Enlist the help of as many competent homeowners as possible. You'll need people to take the lead in such areas as communications, maintenance, insurance, covenants and enforcements, finance, and management. If you have enough support to create committees for each of these key areas, do so. These committee assignments are a good way to identify future community leaders.

Taking over from the developer isn't an event, it's a process. And there are several workable ways to conduct the process. In the early planning stages, the developer established the governing documents for the development, and these probably dictate how your transition will proceed.

You can make the transition gradually and proportionately—as sales increase, non-developer owners gain an increasing number of seats on the board.

You can make the transition at the point where a certain percentage of homes have been sold.

You can make the transition all at once if the developer gives complete control of the association to the homeowners immediately; in this case, the developer will retain veto rights on any board action that would affect the developer's investment.

You can make the transition by electing an interim board of homeowners who would work closely with the developer and represent the interests of the homeowners until the developer completely relinquishes control.

You can make the transition using some combination of these processes.

This is not to suggest that you get to choose how you want to conduct the transition in your association. The structure was established as part of the early planning for the development. The transition period, however, gives you and other homeowners the opportunity to become acquainted with the association's functions and needs before you have to assume complete responsibility.

Your goal is a smooth transfer of authority and responsibility from one large owner of the entire community (the developer) to many individual owners of the entire community. Organization, planning, attention to detail, cooperation, and communication are essential if the process is to play out successfully.

◆ ◆ ◆ ◆

In the past, community associations concerned themselves largely with rules enforcement and facilities management, but more and more associations must rethink their initial agenda and direct their efforts toward building community.

Owners want more out of community association life than warnings about wind chimes or pets. They want to get to know their neighbors, they want a sense of belonging, and they want their community to provide it.

Community is difficult to define, but you know it when you feel it. If you're a self-managing board member, you're undoubtedly deeply imbued with that spirit. Because you're involved with and committed to the community, pursue what you think will benefit the association. In doing so, you will create fellowship, sociability, cooperation, and all the other elements that give your residents a sense of community.

Related Resources

Community First! Emerging Visions Reshaping America's Condominium and Homeowner Associations. Bill Overton, Ed., Community Associations Institute, 1999.
    Self managers who want an idea of the cultural potential of their association, a glimpse into the future of their community, or a unique paradigm on governance will find this collection of essays informative.

Results of the CAI Research Foundation National Survey of Homeowner Satisfaction. Community Associations Institute Research Foundation, 1999.
    The Gallop Organization conducted this survey, which produced some interesting data about the unique character of community associations. Self managers will find it interesting as well as useful for getting a sense of the demographics of their constituents—which may aid with management.

Community Associations Factbook. Community Associations Institute, 1999.
    This resource can give self managers a good idea of how and where the association fits into the larger picture. It provides a useful and interesting comparison of numerous community association demographics.

Transition From Developer Control, 3rd Ed., (GAP Report #3). Amanda G. Hyatt, Community Associations Institute, 1998.
    A thorough discussion of the transition of power and authority between a developer and subsequent individual owners is beyond the scope of *Self-Management;* however, because it's such a critical period in an association's development, self managers might find the additional information in GAP 3 very helpful.

Chapter 2

The Unique Role of a Self-Managing Board

Community association boards are policy-setting bodies. Generally they work with a professional manager that implements those policies; however, self-managing boards fill both roles—leadership *and* management.

The Board's Leadership Role

Like any community association board, your role is to provide the leadership necessary to fulfill the fundamental purpose of the community association—to protect, preserve, and enhance both the physical assets of the association and the quality of life of the residents.

Depending on your governing documents, your role and scope of authority can be broad or specific. Some boards have the same authority as a corporation, some boards have their powers precisely stated, and some don't. Generally, however, boards have the authority to set goals, standards, and policies for the association; to enforce the governing documents; to maintain the property; to maintain the association's financial stability; to purchase adequate insurance; to enter into contracts for services; to create and supervise committees; and to conduct annual meetings and board meetings.

Start with a Good Board

The effectiveness of a board depends on the effectiveness of its individual members, so it's important to start with competent, intelligent, mature people who are willing to work hard and make sacrifices. Your community association is neither a civic league nor a social club. Running it requires making hard decisions and being involved almost on a daily basis. Therefore, candidates should not be selected casually.

When you have your quality board in place, you'll be faced with establishing long-term goals and programs for the association and taking care of current, pressing problems. Obviously, you need to establish priorities.

Attracting Good Board Members Depends On . . .

- The size of the community
- Education and social background of residents
- Economic status of residents
- Average age and health of residents
- Ratio of employed to retired residents
- Ratio of renters to resident owners
- Percentage of families with children

Officer's Roles

Most boards have at least four officers: president, vice president, secretary, and treasurer. If your board is very small, you may have one member wearing two hats—secretary and treasurer, for example.

Each officer has a defined role with requisite tasks and responsibilities. For associations that employ professional management, many of the actual tasks are assigned to the manager while the responsibility remains with the officer. Self-managing boards have the responsibility and the work.

The President: The Leader and Manager of the Association
- Directs the activities of the association
- Motivates and facilitates participation by board members
- Motivates residents to volunteer
- Relies on other board members for guidance and advice
- Assigns or delegates tasks
- Protects and maximizes the association's resources
- Presides at meetings

The Vice President: The President's Backup
- Substitutes for the president when needed
- Conducts or presides at meetings in the president's absence

The Secretary: The Recorder of the Association
- Records the association's activities (minutes)
- Signs official documents
- Maintains records of the association

The Treasurer: The Chief Financial Officer of the Association
- Prepares financial reports
- Maintains association accounts
- Prepares and monitors the association budget
- Analyzes the association reserve accounts to ensure proper funding

Qualities of a Good Board Member

The Board Member You Want	. . . and Don't Want
Good character	Unable to put the welfare of the community first
Strong integrity	Works behind the board to run things his or her own way
Calm judgment	Impulsive or quick tempered
Willingness to serve	Has a personal or hidden agenda
Committed to giving time and effort	Puts individual interests first
Relevant experience or background	Little experience in management
Previous volunteer service	Unable to work with others for the common good
Strong "people skills"	Ineffective with others

Depending on whether you reside in a condominium, planned community, or cooperative, your association's governing documents may specify additional or alternate duties for officers; check them carefully and tailor the list to your situation.

Fiduciary Duty

As a board, and especially as a managing board, you operate in a fiduciary capacity for the homeowners. This simply means that the board makes decisions in the best interests of the association. Most of those decisions will affect service and maintenance in the community.

Your duty of loyalty keeps you from using your position to take advantage of the association. You can't make decisions for the association that benefit your own interests at the expense of the association and its members.

Your duty to exercise ordinary care means that you must perform your duties in good faith, in a manner that you reasonably believe to be in the best interest of the corporation, with such care as an ordinary prudent person in a similar position under similar circumstances would use. In short, you must act in the best interests of the association and act reasonably.

You also need to be concerned with local, state, and national legislative matters that could affect community associations. You'll need to keep an eye on neighboring zoning change applications that could affect the value or livability of your community. You should promote good public relations with the larger community, search for educational opportunities for your members, and work to identify members who would make good future board members.

In your dual role as a self-managing board, you're not only the executive organ of the association with chief responsibility for its well being, but you also have to accomplish all the management functions listed above and more in the best interests of the association's homeowners.

How to Fulfill Your Fiduciary Duty

- Develop and use a formal budgeting process
- Establish and adhere to budgetary guidelines
- Make sure the budgeting process reflects the wishes of the association members
- Promote understanding and acceptance of the reserve accounts among the members
- Collect sufficient fees to adequately operate the association
- Solicit bids and negotiate appropriate contracts
- Authorize expenditures

Making Decisions and Understanding the Business Judgment Rule

When self managing your community, you must use care in making decisions. In fact, you're obligated by law to do so. You'll be judged by a standard known as the business judgment rule to determine if you carried out or breached your duty to the association in making a decision.

The business judgment rule won't apply to all situations. For instance, if you misinterpret your governing documents, the rule won't apply. Similarly, other rules will be used to determine whether the association will be liable for damages. The business judgment rule only considers whether you met your duty of care to the owners as a whole in making your decision.

Using Experts

The law doesn't expect you to know everything on each matter that comes before the board for a decision. However, it does require you to ask someone qualified and knowledgeable in the appropriate field for specialized information in order to make that decision.

For example, when the roof needs to be replaced, you won't be expected to know what type of roofing material is appropriate or what the building code requires. However, you'll be expected to consult with an architect or engineer experienced in replacing roofs and make an informed decision based on the information the expert gives you.

Do you need an expert for every decision? In general, not for the day-to-day operations of the association; but, it depends on the nature and scope of each particular matter. Do you need to consult an "expert" before you undertake the annual touch-up painting using the same paint that you've used successfully for the past ten years where the cost is $5,000 on a $100,000 budget? Clearly, the answer is no. However, if the paint is failing prematurely and the entire complex needs re-painting, certainly obtaining qualified opinions is appropriate.

Do you always need to consult with a professional or hire an expensive consultant? The level of expertise you need depends on the nature and cost of each particular project. In general, you should seek highly trained experts for complex, significant and costly projects. Whereas, in the paint example, you could get advice from three or four reputable painting contractors, and that would likely be sufficient.

Make sure that you get advice not only from someone with the appropriate level of expertise, but from someone who isn't likely to make biased recommendations. For example, you can't expect a paint manufacturer's representative to give you reliable advice about your painting project when he or she is selling a product. Instead, you must consult with independent professionals like engineers, architects, accountants, and lawyers who are only selling their advice. The sales representative is paid only if you chose his or her product. However, professional experts receive no commission if you follow their advice, so their opinions are entitled to more weight.

> **The Business Judgment Rule**
>
> - Did you act within the bounds of your authority?
> - Did you act in good faith?
> - Did you believe that you were acting in the best interest of the association?
> - Did you consult with experts in the relevant field?
> - Did you get enough information?
> - Did you base your decision on what was best for the owners as a whole?

What about insurance? Like many self-managing boards, you may rely solely on the advice of your insurance agent when you decide which policy is appropriate. But your insurance agent is not a professional expert that you hired to work for you. He or she receives a commission from the insurance company on the policies sold.

Perhaps the best approach to buying insurance is to locate a licensed insurance advisor. This person may also be an insurance agent; however, you can hire on a fee basis to develop specifications for your association's insurance needs. You should then ask several agents to bid on these specifications. In that way, you compare apples to apples.

You'll make proper decisions if you get enough reliable information to make a good faith judgment. Hiring appropriate experts or consultants is one way to meet this obligation. The law calls this good business judgment. It's really just good common sense.

Working With Committees

As a volunteer, self-managing board, you may not be able to accomplish everything that you need to do. Consider getting some help from resident committees.

There are two types of committees: ad hoc committees are task oriented and dissolve when the task is completed; standing committees are function oriented and remain in force indefinitely. The parking committee that is tasked with researching the need for additional parking space and making recommendations to the board is an ad hoc committee. The rules committee that hears appeals from residents as needed is a standing committee.

When you form an ad hoc committee, provide *in writing* exactly what the task is, when it should be completed, how many and what kinds of recommendations the board wants from the committee, and how much authority the committee has.

When you form a standing committee, develop a set of guidelines for the structure, function, and responsibility of the committee.

The board or the committee itself should appoint a chair who will direct the committee's work and convey reports to the board. Assign one member of the board as liaison to each committee. The board liaison shouldn't chair the committee or have a vote, but instead serve as an adviser.

The Board's Management Role

As a self-managing board, you not only have a leadership role, you also have the responsibility to oversee the day-to-day operations of the community. You can contract for almost any service that you need; however, you or your resident volunteers will have to do everything else.

Solving Problems

Many of the concerns that will come before the board can roughly be classified into two categories: people and property problems. People problems can usually be resolved with personal attention, but property problems generally require spending money.

Probably most people problems stem from a lack of understanding of the association rules. Too often prospective purchasers are looking only for an easier lifestyle and do not read the association documents before purchasing, or even after purchasing. Try to make some sort of contact with the new residents shortly after they move in to welcome them to the community and to remind them to refer to the association's rules.

In the property category, one source of problems is the construction defects inherited from a developer. These problems can be hidden for a long time. Construction defects are frustrating because the board can't plan for either the timing or the magnitude of the required repair or replacement.

Building components that go bad long before their expected life spans are also troublesome. Can the repair work be spread out and paid for from the present income stream within the operating budget, or is it special assessment time? How about a bank loan? On the positive side, is it time for a special assessment to provide for a desirable community improvement?

Conducting Operations

One of your primary roles is managing the operations of the association. That means you'll be implementing as well as formulating policies, and you'll be the primary contact with residents, contractors, local officials, and others. You'll do your own research when the board needs to be educated on an issue—everything from studying your governing documents to brushing up on facilities maintenance.

Even the most seasoned professional community association manager will turn to outside experts on a regular basis, and the same is true for self-managing boards. You'll need a competent attorney, accountant, insurance agent, and engineer at your disposal. Additionally, you'll want the expert advice of numerous service providers like electricians, plumbers, building contractors, and others. Seeking the advice of outside experts and considering their recommendations when you make decisions for your association is a good management practice. It shows that you've exercised sound business judgment—a fundamental element of your fiduciary duty.

Chapter 5 provides more information about working with professionals and outside experts.

When managing your association, you will face many decisions in the normal course of day-to-day operations. You may be called upon to make emergency repairs on a leaking water pipe or interpret a rule. In all these matters, you must be fair and reasonable and able to justify your decision. You should stay clear of matters where the association has no authority. Some residents will try to bring the association into neighbor-to-neighbor disputes by alleging violations against one another. You should tell the resident that the association does not become involved in such disputes and direct them to other resources or agencies that may be able to help.

Part of your management role is administering the finances of the association; you will want to work closely with the association attorney and accountant, stay within established policies regarding the expenditure of funds, and ensure that you understand them. In all matters of finances, you must always remain above reproach. See chapter 9 for more information on finances.

Other routine operational matters:

- Awarding contracts
- Verifying work is properly done before payment
- Deciding between insurance coverage and the amount of risk the association can afford to assume
- Establishing the need for and cost of professional property inspections
- Deciding on accounting methods (cash, modified cash, or accrual)
- Deciding the best way to collect assessments
- Creating procedures for delinquencies
- Determining cash-flow control
- Improving traffic patterns
- Funding reserves realistically

Working with Residents, Vendors, and Local Officials

In the management role, you'll come in contact with many different types of people—residents, attorneys, accountants, service providers, and sometimes even local elected and government officials.

Since you're the resident's main contact, you'll probably talk to them every day, and sometimes they're going to be upset. You should remain calm, but not accept verbal abuse or threats. Simply tell the resident that their behavior is unacceptable, and ask them to call back or return when they're calm.

You'll also be the main contact for vendors and contractors. You'll oversee their work, conduct inspections, and decide when work is complete and payment due.

Local government officials can provide a lot of information and assistance to community associations. You may want to meet with these officials and discuss how you can work together and assist each another. Establish a cordial relationship even if you don't have an immediate agenda—they'll be helpful when you need to cut through red tape. See chapters 8 and 10 for more information about how to go about this.

◆ ◆ ◆ ◆

Community association board members shoulder a significant responsibility for the governance of their communities. Self managers have the added responsibility of also managing their associations. Through education, relying on experts, and understanding their association's governance and operational needs, they can be successful and fulfilled in this important endeavor.

Related Resources

The Role of the Association Secretary (GAP #18). Shenk & Nagle, Community Associations Institute, 1999.

> Secretaries of self-managed associations have significant responsibilities. Those who want comprehensive information about the nature and scope of those responsibilities and how to accomplish the various tasks associated with them, will find this guide quite useful. It does a good job of outlining the three major functions the secretary must attend to—recording, corresponding, and filing.

The Role of the Association Treasurer (GAP #22). Howard A. Goldklang, Community Associations Institute, 1998.

> Although the title suggests this guide is primarily of interest to association treasurers, the financial information it contains will be of interest to all board members. Even if your association uses the services of a CPA, or if your treasurer is a CPA, all board members—especially in self-managed associations—would be advised to have a basic understanding of community association finances.

The Role of the Association President (GAP #23). Robert T. Dennistoun, Community Associations Institute, 1999.

> Presidents of self-managed associations will be interested in GAP 23 because it expands on much of what is presented in this chapter. The section on governance skills is especially valuable because it not only covers the basics of presiding over the association, but it gets into some of the more challenging areas like enhancing potential in others, promoting volunteerism, and developing the abilities of other board members.

Chapter 3

Association Governing Documents

C ommunity associations are legal entities—usually corporations—that sometimes function like governments and at other times like businesses. They're subject to federal regulations, state laws, local ordinances, case law, secondary mortgage market requirements, and their own governing documents. The association governing documents will be of the greatest immediate concern to self managers, but the other areas are just as important.

Federal Laws

All community associations are regulated to some extent by federal laws. These include the Federal Fair Housing Amendments Act of 1988, the Housing for Older Persons Act of 1995, the Telecommunications Act of 1996, the Federal Fair Debt Collection Practices Act, bankruptcy laws, and laws regarding employment practices. These important laws are addressed more fully in Part III. In addition, rules promulgated by federal agencies, such as the U.S. Department of Housing and Urban Development and the Federal Communications Commission, apply to community association operations.

State Laws

There are state laws that govern creation and operation of community associations. Corporate laws, for profit and not for profit, are generally applicable, and most community associations are required to be incorporated under current state laws, unless specifically excluded by the statute itself. Every state has a condominium act which provides for the establishment of condominiums as legal entities. These acts vary in terms of their complexity. The simplest ones provide for the creation of condominiums. The more complex ones may regulate the development and sale of condominiums; provide protection for purchasers, owners, or tenants; and regulate the general operation of condominiums. Not all states have statutes that provide for the establishment of planned communities or cooperatives. If you're self managing one of these communities, check with an attorney who specializes in community association law to find out which of your state laws apply to it.

Local Ordinances

Local ordinances include fire safety codes, discrimination laws, laws regulating swimming pools and golf courses, and so on. Some states have a Department of Real Estate or a Condominium Bureau that may be the source of some regulations. For example, the California Department of Real Estate and the Florida Bureau of Condominiums have regulations that prohibit certain provisions and require others in the governing documents.

Secondary Mortgage Market

The secondary mortgage market also may be the source of some of the requirements that self managers need to keep in mind. For example, the Federal Housing Administration, the Veterans Administration, the Department of Housing and Urban Development, the Federal Home Loan Mortgage Corporation, the Federal National Mortgage Association, and the Government National Mortgage Association impose a variety of requirements. If the developer wishes to comply with the various requirements of these agencies, he or she will insert specific provisions pertaining to insurance, the distribution of financial statements, and the amendment of the declaration or propriety lease in the governing documents.

Case Law

The decisions of state appellate courts have an impact on the operation of a community association. These decisions are known as case law, and may apply to all community associations within a particular state, depending upon the facts of the individual cases.

Association Governing Documents

Not only are you subject to various federal, state, and local laws, but you're also obligated to govern and self manage your association according to its various governing documents. These documents, which provide the legal foundation for your community association, are actually very useful tools for self managers because they provide specific guidance.

> ### Typical Community Association Governing Documents
>
> - Map, plat, plan, or condominium plan
> - Declaration; master deed; or covenants, conditions & restrictions (CC&Rs) (condo or planned community) or proprietary lease, master lease or occupancy agreement (cooperative)
> - Articles of Incorporation or Articles of Association
> - Bylaws
> - Rules and Regulations
>
> There are other legal documents that have legal significance to owners, but they aren't part of the governing documents. They include deeds, certificates, shares of stock, certificate of membership, public offering statements, or other documents.

Map, Plat, or Plan

State and local laws will determine whether your association requires a document called a map, plat, plan, or condominium plan and they will specify the form and content of this document. This document generally identifies the separate interests owned by each person and the common areas that are owned either by the association or the owners, depending on the type of community.

You must understand (and communicate to the residents) the distinction between areas that are separate (unit, lot, or apartment) and areas that are owned in common or by the association.

Declaration, Master Deed, or Proprietary Lease and Their Covenants and Restrictions

In a planned community or condominium, the declaration (master deed) creates the common scheme for the community. In a cooperative, the proprietary lease, or occupancy agreement, creates the common scheme. These documents contain the covenants or restrictions that regulate the residents' behavior. They bind all the owners in interlocking relationships, establish association responsibilities, and define owners' rights and obligations. For example, covenants or restrictions require the association to maintain the common areas, restrict ways units and common property can be used, restrict age of residents, set policies regarding pets, and apportion ownership interest and expenses.

The law states that the covenants or restrictions "run with the land," and are transferred to subsequent owners. This means that lawful restrictions can be enforced against all residents.

Articles of Incorporation or Association

Community associations that are incorporated have articles of incorporation, which are generally much shorter than the declaration or proprietary lease. They initially create the corporation under state law and define its basic purposes and powers. In some states, condominium and planned community associations are not legally required to incorporate, and these may have articles of association. However, most community associations are incorporated, and all cooperative associations must be.

Your attorney will likely recommend incorporation for your association because it limits individual owners' and directors' liability, entitles the association to exercise the full powers of corporations under state law, and makes it easier for you to deal with other parties.

You should review the articles of your association because they may dictate such things as the number of directors, their terms of office, and other specifics about how you should self manage your association.

Bylaws

Your association bylaws contain provisions concerning actual association operations. Generally, they're developed at the same time as the declaration. Sometimes, they're adopted as soon as a corporation is established. Bylaws address topics such as meetings, procedures for electing the board members and officers, and general duties of the board. They're usually easier to amend than the declaration or proprietary lease.

Resolutions, Rules, and Regulations

Board members adopt rules and regulations, and sometimes members have to approve them. A resolution is a motion that follows a set format and is formally adopted by the board. It must be consistent with the declaration or proprietary lease, the bylaws, and state law.

You should keep an orderly, indexed record of the resolutions adopted by the board (or adopted by committee and approved by the board) in a book of resolutions. Sometimes the declaration and bylaws cover the same topic. For example, your declaration may state that a person must seek the board's approval to own a pet, and your rules allow two pets. If this leads to a problem, courts will generally attempt to construe the documents together and recognize both provisions as valid.

The Hierarchy of Documents

When documents conflict, a court will give the greatest weight to the declaration or proprietary lease, followed by the bylaws, and finally the rules and regulations.

If the articles of incorporation conflict with the bylaws or rules and regulations, the articles of incorporation generally will prevail, but the law varies among the states. Because the articles of incorporation are usually general and concise, the declaration or proprietary lease and articles probably won't conflict. If they do, however, seek legal counsel.

If, for some reason, your governing documents don't comply with the law, they're invalid. Also, if the language in the declaration or lease, articles, or bylaws give residents a particular right, you can't change it by making rules or regulations to the contrary.

The Four Types of Resolutions

1. *Policy resolutions* affect owners' rights and obligations. For example, rules for the use of common areas and recreational facilities, architectural guidelines, or enforcement procedures are established by policy resolutions.

2. *Administrative Resolutions* address the internal operations of the community association. For example: operating procedures, collection procedures, and meeting locations are established by administrative resolution.

3. *Special resolutions* record board decisions that apply a policy or rule to an individual situation. For example, a decision about an alleged rule violation or authorization of a lawsuit would be recorded in a special resolution.

4. *General resolutions* record board decisions regarding routine events. For example, adopting the annual budget or approving a contract would be recorded in a general resolution.

◆ ◆ ◆ ◆

Since your governing documents will probably all agree with one another, understanding them and operating according to the provisions they lay out should be easier than you might think. These documents will provide the structure within which you can work effectively, they'll guide your decision making and support your operations. Their greatest value, however, may lie in the protections they provide to you as a self manager.

Related Resource

Condominium and Homeowner Association Practice: Community Association Law, 3rd Ed., Wayne S. Hyatt. American Bar Association, 2000.

For a more in-depth treatment of the legalities of community association governing documents, Hyatt's book—written for nonlawyers—provides a good understanding of the basics.

Chapter 4

Developing and Enforcing Rules

One of your more sensitive activities as an association board is developing and adopting rules. In your management role, you have the added responsibility of enforcing them. How you go about doing this sets the tone of life within the community.

Developing Rules

When you're developing your rules, or updating old ones, you'll need an appreciation of what the community wants as well as an understanding of what can, and cannot, be regulated. Also, you must have a clear sense of what you want to achieve with your rules and regulations.

Know Your Authority

There are three restrictions on your association: laws, covenants, and rules.

Laws: Legal restrictions are those imposed by governmental authorities. You won't be involved in making or adopting these types of restrictions, but you have an obligation to the owners to ensure that your association enforces

The Three Restrictions on Community Associations

	Laws	Covenants	Rules
Who develops or amends?	Government authorities	Developer originally, then owners by amendment	Board of Directors
Examples	FDCPA, ADA, FHAA	Leasing, occupancy, architecture, voting	Pets, parking, facilities use, window treatments
Board obligations	Awareness, compliance, enforcement	Awareness, compliance, enforcement	Develop, adopt, amend, and enforce
Limitations	None	Federal, state, local law, supercede	Federal, state, local law, and covenants supercede

them where necessary. One way you can do this is to incorporate the more important of these legal restrictions in your association's rules and regulations or in a resident's handbook.

Covenants: Usually the developer establishes the covenant restrictions when the community is created. Owners can subsequently add to or modify them by amending the governing documents.

Your association has a set of governing documents such as covenants, conditions and restrictions (CC&Rs), a declaration of restrictions, a declaration of condominium, a master deed, bylaws, or a proprietary lease depending on whether it's a homeowner's association, condominium, or cooperative. These documents contain various provisions specifying what you can and cannot do. They are generically called covenants or restrictions, and your state's statutes or common law dictate where within your governing documents they must be.

Certain federal and state laws may limit your covenants and restrictions. For instance, you may not discriminate against families with children or the handicapped, even if your covenants and restrictions allow it, because the 1988 Fair Housing Amendments Act and the Americans With Disabilities Act—both federal law—prohibit it.

The major difference between covenants and rules is that a board can make, amend, or rescind the rules but it alone cannot modify the covenants. Only unit owners can modify covenants and restrictions, and they can only do so by amending the governing documents. Usually this requires a specified vote or consent of a certain percentage of owners and, in some cases, mortgage lenders.

Rules: The third restriction on your association is the set of rules and regulations. As a board, you can adopt, amend, or rescind rules and regulations. This is the area where you have the greatest authority—and the greatest responsibility. However, there are a few instances where this authority is limited.

Limits on Your Authority to Make Rules

- In some states rules and regulations can only apply to the use and operation of common areas.
- Sometimes, rules and regulations may be used to expand upon or clarify covenants and restrictions already in the governing documents.
- Sometimes the owners have veto power over board-promulgated rules and regulations.

Know Your Limitations

You must understand the limitations that apply to your situation before you adopt a rule. You'll hamper the effective administration of your community by adopting rules and regulations that cannot be enforced because they exceed the law or your authority to adopt them. If you're unsure about the limitations on your authority to adopt rules, consult your association attorney—before you begin developing rules.

Know Your Goals

Begin with a clear view of what you want to regulate. Make sure you're considering useful rules that serve a purpose, can be enforced, and regulate the least. As a general principle, the law doesn't favor rules that restrict an owner's use of his or her property. If you don't enforce your rules consistently and evenhandedly, the law considers them waived. Therefore, you should avoid adopting rules and regulations that you will not, or cannot, enforce.

Drafting Good Rules

Once you've decided your goals and purposes and reviewed them with your association attorney to ensure that you have the authority to adopt them, you're ready to begin actually drafting rules. Consider forming a rules committee or otherwise seek input from your residents early in the process.

Solve the Right Problem

Make sure you have a clear purpose in mind and that the rule you're considering will accomplish that purpose. In other words, make sure you solve the right problem. For example: although it's a good rule, requiring all pets to be on leashes will not necessarily eliminate dog waste on the common areas. Instead your rule should require dog owners to clean up after their pets.

Make Rules Simple, Clear, and Positive

The best rules are simple and clear; but, most important, they are stated positively. Avoid creating a list of "don'ts." Instead, make every effort to phrase rules in the positive. For example, "Car washing prohibited Mon–Fri" could be stated in the positive as "Cars may be washed only on Saturdays and Sundays from 10:00 a.m. to 4:00 p.m. in the parking lot behind the clubhouse."

Organize Rules in Logical Categories

You'll undoubtedly want to record your rules in a resident's handbook or other form that is easily available to everyone. When you do, group them by category, such as maintenance, common area use, parking, landscaping standards, trash removal, architectural guidelines, recreational facilities, etc. This will make a handy reference document that's easy to use.

Adopting Rules

Before you formally adopt any rule, avoid controversy and problems by circulating a draft among the residents and asking them for comments within a specified time. By including the residents in this way, you reduce discord and opposition. It's time consuming, but it prevents complaints about the board being dictatorial.

While you're under no obligation to accommodate every suggestion, it's a good idea to give serious consideration to the responses you get from residents. Fine tune where possible or eliminate clauses or conditions that are clearly objectionable to the residents. It's likely that objectionable rules won't be followed and will only lead to enforcement problems later. Better to look for acceptable alternatives that achieve your goal. You can also make additions based on suggestions you receive from residents.

Ultimately, you make the decision and adopt the rules, but inviting the residents to comment is imperative.

Adopt by Vote

Once you've considered resident input and finalized your rules, you'll need to vote to formally adopt them; and, in some cases, the owners may have to vote as well. Unless your governing documents require the owners to vote on adopting the rule, you should prepare a resolution stating the rule or regulation and place the adoption on the agenda for a vote at your next meeting. Otherwise, follow the procedures required by your association's governing documents.

> ### How to Adopt New Rules and Regulations
>
> - Get resident feedback on rules under consideration. Circulate a final draft of the proposed rules or rule amendments to the residents for comment. Specify a due date and provide a mechanism for residents to respond—a phone number to call, a questionnaire to complete, or a request for a written response.
>
> - Give serious consideration to the responses of the residents. Consider abandoning a rule that residents find objectionable. Make changes where possible as requested by residents, but remember you are under no obligation to incorporate every comment.
>
> - Draft the final rule in the form of a resolution and adopt it by formal vote of the board.

Publishing and Recording Rules

After you've formally adopted the rules and regulations, you must distribute them to the owners and residents. Your work up to this point will be of little value if you don't let the residents know what the new rules are. Furthermore, you may not be able to enforce rules you haven't published. You cannot assume that owners and residents know about rules and regulations that you've adopted, so you should send a copy of the rules with a letter to all owners and residents. Tell your members how important it is to adhere to the rules in order for everyone to enjoy the community.

The last thing you need to do in developing and adopting your rules is to record them at the appropriate registry of deeds or similar governmental office. There's a doctrine called "constructive notice" that says that owners and residents have received notice of restrictions if those restrictions have been recorded or filed with the proper governmental office. You can avoid arguments over whether an owner or resident received notice if you have properly recorded the new rules and regulations. Although this is an important and necessary step, it doesn't substitute for proactively circulating the rules to all residents—something you should do continuously.

Enforcement

Once the rules and regulations are in place, you have to enforce them. You must find a middle ground between being over-zealous on the one hand and resolving violations effectively on the other. You must also avoid being heavy-handed, since this will only fuel controversy in a community. For instance, don't impose fines for minor transgressions, especially for a first offense. This doesn't mean that you shouldn't pursue violations. If you don't enforce your rules, you can face as many problems as enforcing them too aggressively. Instead, find the middle ground.

Some of the rules you should have developed when you were in the drafting and adopting stage are rules for enforcing rules. These are administrative rules that specify how you'll handle rule violations. Consider a multi-step process for enforcement.

Start with a simple personal visit. Particularly in small communities, a phone call or a knock on the door with a friendly reminder and an appeal for compliance may be all that's needed. You may find that the resident is genuinely unaware of a particular rule or that there are extenuating circumstances to be considered—perhaps something the association can help with. This promotes a sense of community and fosters cooperation among residents who will see you as a caring neighbor and leader rather than an enforcer.

If this approach doesn't work, or if you're unable to reach the resident, send a friendly, polite letter explaining the violation. If the resident takes no action to correct the problem, then send a warning. The warning should be more formal and reference the information in the earlier letter. It should also set a deadline for compliance and explain the consequences of noncompliance.

When the friendly and informal approach fails, it may be time to impose fines or suspend privileges. For the most part, community associations have the right to assess fines as part of their powers to enforce covenants and rules, but the right is by no means universal. Check with your association attorney if you are unsure what fines you can or cannot impose.

Due Process

If you impose fines, you'll need to provide for due process. Generally, you can't take action against anyone unless you've

---

Steps to Take Before You File a Lawsuit

1. Pay a personal visit either by phone or in person. Determine that the resident knows about the rule and whether there's anything the association needs to consider about the case.

2. Send a friendly written reminder. State the rule and document the alleged violation.

3. Send a warning. Refer to the reminder that was sent earlier, repeat the information it contained, set a deadline for compliance, and indicate the consequences of noncompliance. Provide an opportunity for due process by scheduling a hearing and inviting the resident's attendance.

4. Impose a fine or suspend privileges. Again, provide an opportunity for due process by offering a hearing.

5. Engage the services of a mediator or consider alternative dispute resolution instead of litigation.

given them an opportunity to explain themselves. Notify the resident in writing, stating the charges, and schedule a hearing that allows time for the resident to prepare. If the board serves as "jury," engage an independent party to conduct the hearing. Notify the resident in writing of the board's decision as soon after the hearing as possible.

Your state may not require a hearing before taking action, but give the resident the opportunity to request a hearing anyway. Include it in the fine notice. Usually, residents don't respond, and you have avoided a hearing that no one attends. However, the advantage to you is that if you end up in court and the resident complains that there was no hearing, you can note that one was offered and not requested. More often than not this is adequate.

How to Conduct a Hearing

Do

- Keep it simple and informal.
- State the case against the resident.
- Let the resident respond in his or her own words.
- Listen carefully to the resident's explanation
- Require complainants to attend the hearing.
- Obtain compliance

Don't

- Don't use a court-like setting or procedure.
- Don't engage in argument
- Don't confront or cross examine the resident
- Don't ask questions unless you need clarification
- Don't act on anonymous complaints that place the association in the role of accuser
- Don't inflict punishment

Conduct a Hearing

If your state requires hearings, you need to follow required procedures. Otherwise, keep your hearing simple and informal.

Avoid the temptation to create a court-like setting or procedure. Give the resident an opportunity to explain, and limit yourself to asking questions only if you need clarification. You should never engage the resident in an argument. Make every effort to reach an understanding. Bear in mind that your goal is to have the residents abide by the rules, not to punish them or enrich the association by collecting fines.

When you're conducting a hearing, due process merely requires a fair procedure, not necessarily a court-type proceeding. You have no right to confront or cross-examine. However, if the violation is based on a complaint, such as excessive noise, then you should require the complainant to lodge the complaint in writing and appear at the hearing to present his or her side of the story. Don't let your board be put in the position of accuser by acting on anonymous complaints. If a resident is unwilling to stand behind their complaint, then you shouldn't get involved.

Suspend Privileges

Suspending privileges instead of imposing fines can be a very effective tool. You may get a resident's attention and compliance much faster by suspending a pool or parking pass than by sending a fine notice in the mail. If you chose this method, make sure you monitor and enforce it, and remember that due process applies in this case also.

If the fines go unpaid, you *may* be able to place a lien on the unit. Some declarations allow liens only for nonpayment of assessments, not fines, so review your declaration and state statute carefully. Also, your declaration will dictate whether you can collect attorneys' fees, late charges, and interest when taking legal action for nonpayment of fines.

Mediation and Alternative Dispute Resolution

If monetary and other incentives fail to get results, you may be ready to go to court. When problems persist, instead consider engaging the services of a mediator—either paid or volunteer—before pursuing litigation.

In mediation, a neutral third party trained in conflict resolution meets with representatives of the association and the resident to persuade each to settle their differences voluntarily. This person is skilled at identifying the underlying source of contention, finding a middle ground, and negotiating a resolution that's acceptable to everyone.

Mediation can keep minor conflicts from becoming major court battles and, thus, reduce expenses for everyone. More important, it also reduces ill will, bad feelings, and possibly a divided community. Even if mediation doesn't keep you out of court, it can clarify the real issues, contribute to a pre-trail settlement, present settlement options, or provide significant information to both parties.

Mediators can be found in the yellow pages and through the court system (try the clerk of the small-claims court or the local district attorney's office). Many communities have nonprofit organizations that provide mediation services at little or no cost.

Another option that you might want to consider before you pursue litigation is arbitration. Decisions reached in arbitration are as final and binding as a court decision; however, the procedures are informal, the costs are reasonable, the parties get to pick the arbitrator, the hearings are private, and the process is generally efficient. Contact the American Arbitration Association for information and referrals.

Going to Court

When all else fails, then you file a lawsuit. Some states require mediation, and others require arbitration. In most cases, however, you must resort to a lawsuit.

You will first ask the court to issue an injunction that requires the resident to comply with the rule, regulation, or restriction. You will also seek a judgment from the court declaring that the fines are due and must be paid. You may also ask the court to require the resident to pay your attorney's fees. These are the most common legal remedies, but your governing documents must contain the appropriate provisions for your type of community in order for you to use them.

◆◆◆◆

You must be consistent and even handed if you want to succeed at enforcing the rules. You must remember that your goal is to get residents to comply with the rules, regulations, and restrictions. Punishment is not your domain, nor should it be. Your role is to foster a congenial, respectful community. Crafting your association's rules properly and enforcing them wisely will go a long way toward ensuring this.

Related Resources

Be Reasonable, How Community Associations Can Enforce Rules Without Antagonizing Residents, Going to Court or Starting World War III. Kenneth Budd, Community Associations Institute, 1998.

> The delicate balance between enforcing rules and maintaining community harmony is explored from several angles in this popular book. Self managers struggling with enforcement issues or those who are stuck with outdated or unreasonable restrictions should find it helpful.

Drafting Association Rules, Gurdon H. Buck. (GAP Report #7). Community Associations Institute, 1996.

> This guide makes drafting good rules a relatively straightforward process. Of particular interest, however, is the 10-page sample rule book contained as an appendix to the guide.

Writing & Enforcing Parking Rules for Community Associations, Community Associations Institute, 1996.

> This book is useful for its many sample documents—bylaw parking provisions, rules, parking space license agreement, letters to residents, violation notices and logs, vehicle information form, and others.

Alternative Dispute Resolution and Consensus Building, Mary Avgerinos. (GAP Report #26), Community Associations Institute, 1997.

> Much has been written by social psychologists about conflict management, but little has been focused on self-managed community associations. The unique challenge in this arena is balancing your effectiveness as a policy setting body with your need to manage daily operations and deal with the conflict that inevitably arises. Self managers will appreciate this guide's approach to managing conflict within the community association environment. Also, the numerous sample documents in the appendix provide good practical tools for self-managed associations.

Pet Policies: How To Draft and Enforce Rules That Sit, Stay, and Heel. Debra H. Lewin. (GAP Report #28), Community Associations Institute, 2001.

> Besides the considerations raised by the fair housing act about service animals, the larger issue of regulating pets in community associations seems to be an ongoing question. GAP 28 discusses this question at some length and offers solutions and ideas that self managers may find helpful.

Part II: Areas of Operation

Chapter 5

Working With Professionals

As a self-managing board you will be responsible for managing every aspect of your association's operations, and using outside experts should be an integral part of your management strategy. Board and committee members change periodically and commitment levels vary, therefore these professionals provide continuity and stability. In addition, whether you consulted a qualified expert is one of the things you will be judged by—should anyone ever question your decisions. (See chapter 2 for details on decision making and the business judgment rule.)

There are a few basic procedures that you should employ regardless of what type of consultant, expert, or contractor you hire, and there are a few specific things you should know about your primary professional partners—the attorney, accountant, reserve specialist, and insurance agent.

Finding the Right One

Decide what you need. Make a list, include the volume of work for each item on the list, and prioritize it. In some cases this list may develop into a specification that you would use to solicit bids. In other cases, it may simply help you decide whether to pay a professional on an hourly basis or put them on retainer—a flat monthly fee. Share your list with all prospective candidates, and ask them if there is anything they would add to it.

Find the right people. Finding professionals who are knowledgeable about and specialize in community associations can be challenging, but it's vital that your professional partners understand your unique needs. The Yellow Pages won't have a subheading for community associations, but there are other good sources who can provide names of the people you'll want to work with. The local chapter of the Community Associations Institute is the best place to start. Other community associations in your area are another good source of referrals—particularly those that work with a professional manager. Managers are an excellent source of information about professionals who specialize in community associations because they work with many of them daily. If you have already hired one professional like an accountant, for instance, that person can likely refer you to appropriate attorneys, reserve specialists, or insurance professionals because they're all working in the same industry and tend to know one another.

Contact several prime candidates. Share your list of needs, and invite candidates to submit a proposal or letter of interest. Decide on two or three and invite them to meet with you for an interview. The sections below provide somewhat more detailed information on this part of the process for each professional you will work with.

Check references. Always ask for at least three references. Prepare four or five key questions, pose the same questions to each reference, and compare the responses. Don't rely on the references to make your decision for you—use the information you receive to confirm a decision you've already made or to help you decide between two equally acceptable candidates. Also, ask other professionals, such as attorneys or engineers, for information about your chosen candidate. Use this information to confirm that you made the best choice.

Get everything in writing. Always sign a contract for services with outside experts, vendors, and consultants. When you ask for a recommendation or opinion from one of them, get it in writing. This eliminates misinterpretations, contains costs, and is just good business practice.

Assign one person as the primary contact. Once you've made your selection and signed a contract, decide who will be the association liaison or contact person for that professional. An attorney or accountant is not going to serve the association effectively if he or she has to communicate with four or five people who may have differing levels of knowledge. The treasurer might be the primary contact for the association accountant, the president for the attorney, and the facilities committee chair for the electrical contractor. Be sure to assign a backup also.

> ### Where to Get Referrals of Qualified Professionals
>
> - Call the local chapter of CAI for the names of certified community association professionals.
> - Ask other community associations in your area who they work with. Contact their manager if they have one.
> - Ask other professionals already working for your association.
> - Contact the local or state office of the appropriate professional organization, such as the bar association or CPA society.
> - Contact your state licensing organization. If it recognizes a real estate or association specialization, it may have a directory of members.
> - Consult the professional directory at www.caionline.org.

The Attorney

There are nearly a million licensed attorneys in the United States at the beginning of the 21st century. Finding one that specializes in community association law and fits the unique needs of your community association requires you to be informed and organized. The more organized your search, the more successful you are likely to be.

Create a small team to interview candidates. As a self-managed board, you will be working closely with the attorney you select, so you want to select someone you are comfortable with. Therefore, more than one member of the board should be on the team. You may want to also include homeowners or others who are not on the board, but who can share useful opinions and impressions.

Make appointments to visit each candidate for a consultation during regular business hours in his or her office. Take note of how far in the future the consultation is set—this may be an indication of how accessible the attorney will be in the future. At the time you make the appointment, ask that literature about the firm be mailed to you. Also ask for samples of billing statements, monthly status reports, legal opinion letters or other relevant documents. Also, ask for references from other community association clients.

Look for professionalism and timeliness. During your consultation, observe the professionalism and timeliness of the attorney and the legal staff. For instance, was your team kept waiting?

Be candid and informative. Let the attorney know that you are "shopping," and that you will be interviewing more than one candidate. Give the candidate the list you compiled of your association's needs. Include on the list the name and phone number of one member of the team who will be the primary contact for the attorney.

What Attorneys Do For Community Associations

Collect delinquent assessments: Write and send routine demand letters, file liens, process foreclosures, litigate if necessary.

Enforce deed restrictions: Write and send routine demand letters, file lawsuits, litigate if necessary

Litigate: For collections, to enforce deed restrictions, to defend the Board.

Review documents: Review governing documents, rules proposed by the board, or contracts with other service providers.

Provide legal opinions: Advise the board in all matters pertaining to the association.

Educate: Attend meetings to answer questions, explain concepts or documents, and provide information to homeowners or board members.

Interview Questions for the Attorney

Develop a standard set of questions to pose to prospective attorneys during an interview. Place the most important questions first in case you don't get through all the questions. Consider questions covering the following areas.

Personnel: Ask about the attorney's education and experience—especially in community association matters. Ask whether the attorney employs any associates. How many paralegals and other support staff would be available to service your account?

Documents: Review with the attorney the billing statements, monthly status reports, legal opinion letters or other sample documents that you received prior to the consultation. Ask that the billing rate and type of billing be fully explained. Make sure you understand and find acceptable the reports and legal opinion letters.

Qualifications: Ask the attorney what certifications he or she may have. For example, your state may require board certification. Ask whether the attorney specializes in community association law or is a member of CAI. Ask what percentage of the practice is devoted to association law and the type of community association issues typically addressed.

Billing: Ask if it is standard procedure for an assignment to be given to the lowest-billing person when possible. Ask questions about hourly rates, retainers, and direct costs.

After your team has interviewed all the candidates, discuss the results. These will vary from attorney to attorney and from law firm to law firm, so you will be comparing apples to oranges—however unavoidably. Focus on the differences, and see how important those areas are to the unique needs of your association. Rank your list and select the candidate you believe best fits the association and the personalities of the board members.

Once you've made your decision, contact each attorney you interviewed, and let them know you've made a decision. Ask the one you selected to draw up a detailed engagement letter (a contract between the association and the law firm) that sets out the hourly fees for all billable personnel (including minimum billing increments). If you decide not to pay by the hour, ask for a list of standard fees such as the cost of a first demand letter, for a second demand letter, or the cost of filing an original petition. Also, ask how direct costs such as copying and faxing are billed.

Review your new attorney's performance periodically. Make sure that you and the attorney each understand what is expected. Don't settle for second best. If you and the other members of the board are not satisfied, begin the search again until you find the best legal counsel for your association.

The Accountant

Before you embark on your search for the right accountant for your community association, you need to be aware that there are different types of accountants. They can be sole practitioners or associates in a large firm. They can be pubic accountants (PCs) or certified public accountants (CPAs). CPAs are licensed by the state, and only they are qualified to perform audits. CPA firms are monitored by peer review, and you should ask for a copy of the last peer review from any firm you are considering hiring. Since only a CPA can perform the services required by your governing documents, you will want to make sure you select this type of professional.

Compile a list of qualified candidates. The most important things you can look for when making a list of prospective accountants is experience and proper credentials. Begin by contacting the local chapter of CAI, and ask for the names of qualified members in your area. You can also contact your state CPA Society for names of accountants who specialize in common-interest realty associations (CIRAs). And, you might ask your association attorney or engineer for the names of accountants they hold in high regard. As you compile your list of prospective candidates, consider the size and location of the firm, its accessibility, and the personality of the associates. Only add to your list those who meet your criteria.

Meet with and interview qualified candidates. Your board should meet with prospective candidates either during a regularly scheduled meeting or by visiting their offices. Explain your volunteer and staff capabilities and let the candidate know what your needs are, especially if your association is in special circumstances such as litigation. Ask questions about services and fees and other matters of interest to you, and ask for references.

Sign a contract. Ask your new accountant for an engagement letter that lists services and fees in detail. Decide whether hourly rates or fixed fees are best for your association. Hourly rates are appropriate for ongoing services like keeping the books, and fixed fees are best for finite services such as conducting the annual audit. Review the letter carefully, and ask the accountant to clarify any items that are not entirely clear and acceptable to you.

What Accountants Do For Community Associations

Provide Written Reports

- Audits and transition audits
- Compilations
- Expert testimony and litigation support
- Tax returns
- Reviews
- Budgets
- Reserve studies
- Performance reports

Provide Services

- Develop accounting policies and procedures
- Create accounting policies and procedures manual
- Design and implement systems for internal control
- Formulate investment policies
- Evaluate, select, and install accounting software
- Train bookkeepers and other accounting staff
- Prepare monthly or quarterly financial statements
- Make recommendations for interviewing and hiring accounting personnel

Consult and Advise

- Educate and train board or committee members on technical matters
- Make presentations at meetings
- Evaluate and explain work of other professionals such as engineers
- Evaluate and advise on replacement funding strategies
- Advise on budgets and long-term financial plans
- Assist in obtaining financing
- Answer technical questions
- Provide business and financial advice

How to Work Effectively with Your Accountant

Regard the relationship as long term. The advantage to developing a long-term relationship with an accountant is that is provides consistency and historical perspective for new board members and volunteers.

Know what you want. There are two types of services your accountant can provide to the association—required and discretionary. Your governing documents will tell you which is which for your association. For instance, audits and financial statements are usually required, and your documents will specify the requirements for the audit or state when the financial statements should b completed. On the other hand, if you are assuming management from a developer or management company, you may want additional discretionary services. Specialized discretionary services might be needed if your association is facing potential litigation or finds itself in unusual circumstances

Define the accountant's role. Consider the capabilities and roles of the volunteers who will work with the accountant such as the board, the treasurer, or the finance committee. Are there gaps you want the accountant to fill? Who will the accountant work with most directly—treasurer or finance chair? Answering these questions will help you and your accountant define roles, responsibilities, and expectations for each person involved.

Set a schedule. Let the accountant know when work is to be completed and when reports such as financial statements should be delivered to the board. Similarly, ask the accountant when he or she needs certain documents from you in order to complete services, particularly audits, reviews and compilations. If you gather these documents for the accountant, it may save time, and perhaps lower the audit fees. Include on the schedule a date for the accountant to meet with you to discuss the audit results. Ask for this in writing and ask the accountant to include his or her observations of or comments about conditions you should be aware of.

The accountant is a vital part of your association's professional team. Success requires that you know what the accountant does, how you can benefit from the accountant's capabilities, and what you want and need. As you develop a long-term relationship with your accountant, your community will benefit from his or her advice, industry expertise, and wisdom.

The Reserve Specialist

From time to time your association needs to replace some very expensive common elements such as a roof. You must set aside enough money each year for that roof so that when the time comes to replace it, you have the funds to cover it. How do you know how long the roof will last? How do you know how much the new roof will cost at that time in the future? A reserve specialist can answer these questions.

The reserve specialist will prepare a reserve study that provides you with guidance on how to keep your association's physical assets from deteriorating faster than your financial assets increase. That study will include an inventory of items that need to be replaced, as estimate of the useful remaining life of these items, an estimate of the cost to replace them, and a plan for funding the replacement.

The reserve specialist cannot prepare a reserve study without your help. He or she will need information such as records of past projects, the most recent reserve balance, and the rate of reserve contributions. Additionally, you can provide information on the current condition of certain major components that may not be obvious.

Types of Reserve Studies

Full reserve studies and update reserve studies are the most common approaches to analyzing your community's future needs. A full reserve study includes a site visit, and an update study may or may not. If your association hasn't conducted a reserve analysis, or hasn't had an older analysis updated recently, you should begin with a full reserve study and maintain it with periodic update studies.

For a full reserve study, the reserve specialist will visit and inspect your community carefully. He or she will prepare an inventory of all components, assess the conditions, estimate the life and value of the common elements, analyze the reserve fund status, and recommend future funding. During the on-site inspection, the reserve specialist will evaluate all the association's common elements to determine which should be included in the reserve component list by answering four questions:

1. Is it a common area maintenance responsibility?
2. Is the component life limited?
3. Does the component have a predictable life limit?
4. Is the replacement cost above a minimum threshold level?

In an update reserve study, the reserve specialist will also visit and inspect your community, assess the condition of the existing inventory, estimate the life and value of the common elements, analyze the status of your reserve funds, and recommend a plan for future funding. However, this study takes less time than the full reserve study because the reserve specialist will only re-evaluate items on the reserve component list and will only spot check a few quantities for accuracy.

The reserve specialist can also complete an update reserve study without a site visit. For this update, the reserve specialist adjusts the life and value of the existing inventory and funds.

The reserve specialist has the expertise and experience to accurately determine the life cycles of your association's components. He or she can evaluate not only physical deterioration (the surface of the tennis court is chipped or cracking), but also aesthetic decay (the recreation room looks like a 1960s movie set) and technological obsolescence (the intercom still works, but replacement parts are no longer available). In addition, the reserve specialist also has a number of resources with which to develop appropriate repair or replacement cost estimates.

In addition to evaluating the physical components of your association, the reserve specialist is also expert in analyzing the financial resources needed to maintain the common elements over time. The reserve specialist balances the size of the reserve fund against the deterioration of the reserve components in the reserve funding plan.

Your association's physical assets are constantly decaying, but the reserve studies prepared regularly by your reserve specialist will provide you with the information you need to protect these assets.

The Insurance Agent

Insurance agents, like doctors and lawyers, have a broad range of specialties and areas of expertise. Fortunately for self-managers, insurance specifically for community associations is one of them. Community associations have unique needs and exposures, so you must select an agent with experience in this area.

Once you have selected your insurance agent, vest in that person and his or her firm the same confidence you have in your attorney and accountant. When you establish and maintain a successful, long-term relationship with your agent, you contribute to the stability and security of your association and to the success of its asset protection plan.

Your insurance agent should be an advocate and a resource. If you select someone who has worked with community associations, you can expect an extra measure of professionalism and experience. Developing a positive working relationship with your agent

> ### How to Find the Right Insurance Agent for Your Association
>
> - Select an agent who can demonstrate that he or she knows the community association field. For example, ask the agent to explain why directors and officers liability insurance is important or what importance fidelity and building ordinance coverages have to your association.
> - Select an agent who has the resources to provide the best products available and the unique services needed by associations.
> - Select an agent who insures other community associations.
> - Select an agent with several years of experience.
> - Select an agent whose community association references report good relationships and high levels of satisfaction.

improves the chances of meeting everyone's need.' For more information about community association insurance, see chapter 10.

◆ ◆ ◆ ◆

You don't have to do it all yourself; in fact, there are some areas where it's preferable to get professional help. Self managers shouldn't hesitate to get the professional support you need—owners and residents will be glad you did. And always remember to work with professionals who are experienced with community associations!

What Insurance Agents Do For Associations

- Review the association's documents, recommend the legal minimum insurance requirements, and recommend additional coverage that might be appropriate.
- Inspect the community physical layout and amenities and identify exposure that needs to be addressed.
- Verify the property values for replacement and/or reproduction costs. This can be accomplished through an appraisal service, a company survey or various others means.
- Review the association's fidelity bond, and ensure that all parties (board members, committee members) with access to the association's assets are included in the definition of an employee.
- Discuss the lending institution guidelines for selecting a bond limit if it is not specified in the association's documents.
- Obtain premium quotations, and help the board select the program that best suits the association's needs.
- Explain to the board, in plain English, the coverage being offered as well as the exclusions and limitations of each.
- Educate the residents about the association's policy. Explain where the association's coverage stops and residents' responsibilities begin.
- Offer the unit owners special coverage and reduced rates.
- Provide certificates of insurance or evidence of coverage to lenders in a timely manner.
- Assist the board in drafting a resolution for processing claims deductibles.
- Create a claims procedure manual that specifies
    How claims are to be reported
    What constitutes an emergency repair
    Which companies have been pre-approved to respond to emergencies
    Which contractors have been pre-approved
    How owners should coordinate a claim between the association's carrier and their own, how the deductible will be handled, what time periods are reasonable for various steps in the claim, and what can be done if the board's expectations are not met.
- Customize a risk-management program that addresses
    Regular site inspections for hazardous conditions
    Safety regulations for recreation facilities
    Washing-machine hose and hot-water heater replacement programs
    Chimney inspection and cleaning guidelines
    How to winterize vacant units and hose bibs
    Procedures for clubhouse rentals
- Assist the association to establish procedures for service providers
    Review certificates of insurance
    List clauses to include in standard contracts (hold harmless agreements and listing the association as an additional insured).
- Review the association's claims annually and recommend how the association can reduce similar future claims.

Related Resources

How to Select & Use Association Legal Counsel (GAP Report #13). Hindman & Jordan, Community Associations Institute, 1998.

> An attorney with experience in community association law will be one of the self-managing association's most important partners. Finding the one that's right for your association and working effectively with that person will be a little easier after reading the practical advice contained in GAP 13. As with many of the GAP reports, this one contains numerous sample documents that provide self managers with interview questions, answers to billing questions, guidance with RFPs, and other practical considerations.

Community Association Insurance: A Guide for Condominium, Cooperatives, and Planned Communities, 4th Ed. (GAP Report #4), Treese & Rosenberry. Community Associations Institute, 1997.

> Self managers seeking in-depth information about community association insurance will find this resource particularly helpful. It answers important questions you might not think to ask. The section on property insurance is particularly useful because it examines the ever-vexing question of common element and limited common element overlap. It also provides information on owner's insurance— not necessarily an association responsibility, but very informative for a self manager.

Community Association Risk Management, 3rd Ed., (GAP Report #25), Clifford J. Treese, Community Associations Institute, 1998.

> An important part of protecting association assets is a good risk management program. This guide picks up where GAP 4 leaves off and discusses important considerations that should be integrated with the association's insurance program. Self managers will be especially interested in the discussions of the management obligations to plan, organize, lead, and control.

A Complete Guide to Reserve Funding and Reserve Investment Strategies, 5th Ed., (GAP Report #24), Frumkin & Juall, Eds., Community Associations Institute, 2001.

> The importance of maintaining adequate reserves can't be overstated. This chapter only touches on the subject, but it deserves thorough study by self managers. GAP 24 provides the in-depth information that is beyond the reach of *Self-Management;* self managers will find it an invaluable component in their community association education.

Conducting Meetings

M eetings are an integral part of management, and whether they're productive and pleasant depends on whether they're conducted efficiently.

Prepare Ahead of Time

One way to keep meetings productive (and from lasting past the point where good decisions can be made) is to provide as much information beforehand as possible. Prepare and distribute packets of information several days before the meeting. It takes time to assemble the materials, but packets allow everyone to arrive prepared to get to work and take action.

A basic meeting packet should include minutes from the previous meeting, committee reports, relevant recent correspondence, and the agenda. Depending on how you operate your association, you may also include other types of information like financial reports or maintenance status updates. Organize the meeting packet in the same order as the agenda. The agenda should include enough detail to prepare participants for possible discussions. Instead of just listing "Treasurer's Report" on the agenda, also list the highlights of the report—especially those that will generate discussion. For example:

Discussion items for upcoming budget preparation.
- Board's input re: user fee increases
- Board's priorities for capital acquisitions
- Projections of annual costs.

The agenda should list the time allocated for each item. More important items like a budget discussion should be given more time. Indeed, one basic rule is that the more money is associated with an item, the more time it gets on the agenda. How long your meetings last will depend to some extent on the size of your association, the number and complexity of management issues, whether you combine governing and management discussions in one meeting, and how often you meet. But it will depend to a greater extent on how well prepared the board is and how well the meeting is conducted.

Whatever your circumstances, if you assemble adequate materials prior to the meeting and plan carefully, you can keep meeting time to a minimum.

Parliamentary Procedure

When self-managing boards meet, they often have their sleeves rolled up and their management hats on. In these circumstances, parliamentary procedure may or may not be helpful. However, when you have your governing hat on and you're representing the stock holders—the owners in the association—it's best to operate under a few basic ground rules.

You can maintain order, keep the meeting moving, and achieve a positive outcome by using parliamentary procedure, and you don't necessarily have to observe every aspect of the highly formalized process outlined in *Robert's Rules of Order*. The important thing is to remember the basic principles underlying the concept of parliamentary procedure:

- Follow the agenda.
- Discuss one subject at a time.
- Give each participant a chance to speak.
- Speak only on the issue being discussed.
- Speak only when recognized by the chair.
- Address questions and comments to the chair.
- Decide issues through motions, seconds, and votes.

Getting Outside Help

Occasionally, the services of a professional meeting facilitator or parliamentarian can be very useful.

Meeting facilitators minimize disruptions and keep the meeting on the agenda by using rules of order. There are a couple of advantages to using a meeting facilitator. First, the facilitator frees a board member or officer from the responsibility of maintaining order and allows them to focus on and contribute to the discussion. Second, by having a skilled facilitator conduct the meeting, the influence of strong biases or dominant participants is minimized. Or the board may simply need a facilitator to provide some initial guidance or basic education on how to do a good job conducting the meeting themselves.

Depending on your size or particular needs, a professional parliamentarian can also be very useful. This person must be familiar with the association's bylaws, standing rules, and procedures, as well as the minutes of the last meeting. A parliamentarian might be appropriate, for example, at an annual owners' meeting, especially if a complex issue like amending the bylaws is being discussed and decided.

It isn't the parliamentarian's job to control the meeting, but rather to advise those conducting the meeting on maintaining the order of business. He or she may be fairly passive, offering advice only when questioned, or may become an active participant, speaking to the assembled members and explaining opinions.

Minutes

Meeting minutes are an association's only official record of its board, committee, or member decisions and actions, so getting them right is important. That doesn't mean they have to be stuffy or cumbersome. Strive for a clear and concise writing style that makes them inviting to the average member.

Publishing minutes isn't required, but it's a good way to let your community residents know how hard you're working and what you're doing. Include them in your newsletter as a regular feature, and if you don't have enough space for complete minutes, at least list actions taken. Also, make minutes available to any association member upon request.

Distribute minutes of all meetings—especially annual meetings—as soon after the event as possible. Then approve them at the next meeting and add copies to your corporate record book.

Elements of Good Meeting Minutes

Good meeting minutes will record the following key elements:

- Type of meeting: Record whether it was a regular, special, adjourned regular, or adjourned special meeting.

- Association name: Record the association's corporate name and the words "Minutes of the meeting of (name of body)."

- Event information: Record the time, date, and place of the meeting.

- Attendees' names: List the names of directors, officers, committee representatives, members, and other key participants.

- Approval of the previous minutes: Unless the assembly waives the reading of the minutes, they should be read and approved or corrected. If corrections are necessary, the board should approve the minutes as corrected.

- Officer and committee reports: Reports often precede the business of the meeting. If they are presented in writing, they can simply be appended to the minutes with board approval. If not, only the fact that the report was made must be recorded.

- The business of the meeting: The minutes should follow the agenda, unless the board agrees to take a matter out of order. There is no reason to include summaries of debates because they do not constitute official action of the assembly.

- The vote: If the vote is "without objection" it should be noted in the minutes. If the vote is by voice, only the chair's ruling needs to be noted by stating "the motion passed." If standing, a show of hands, or a paper ballot divides the assembly, the count should be recorded. For small assemblies, you can record the names of those abstaining, voting in favor of, or in opposition to resolutions and motions. It is important to list those dissenting so that if they disagree, they are not held responsible for the consequences.

- Adjournment: The last paragraph should state the time of adjournment.

- Secretary's signature: "Submitted by (secretary's signature)" should end the minutes.

Types of Meetings

Meetings provide an excellent vehicle for communication, but different needs call for different types of meetings.

Board Meetings

The regular meeting of your board is one of the primary opportunities you have to discuss and set policy, review operations, resolve disputes, listen to residents, and plan for the future. Often the health and harmony of an entire community is directly linked to how constructive these meetings are.

It's imperative that your board meetings be productive, orderly, and free of disruptions. If board members are unskilled in conducting meetings effectively, consider using a trained facilitator, professional parliamentarian, or a neutral party with experience in conducting meetings to conduct business while the president or other officer presides.

Community association board meetings should always be open to members and residents. However, this doesn't mean they may participate; they may only observe, unless asked by the meeting chair to address the board. Create a "homeowner's forum" or "open discussion" as a regular item on your agenda that gives residents an opportunity to address the board. Establish a time limit, and apply it equally to each speaker. Residents whose issues can't be resolved within the time limit should be asked to address the board in writing.

Executive Sessions and Closed Meetings

Closed meetings are not only illegal, they promote distrust and antagonism. Executive sessions are the exception, of course, but the law generally limits the business that can be conducted this way to pending litigation, personnel issues, and contract negotiations. Check your state's statute because laws vary from state to state.

Include an executive session on the agenda if you know you're going to have one, or announce it at the beginning of the meeting. That way, attendees are less likely to be offended when they're asked to leave a meeting. You should also announce the purpose of the executive session, e.g., "to discuss pending litigation," though you don't have to specify any further details. Only the discussion takes place in executive session—you will need to reconvene in open session to take a vote.

Even if a meeting is closed, its *results* should be recorded in the minutes—only the discussion is confidential. For example, the minutes may record that during an executive session, the board discussed a disputed contract and reached a satisfactory resolution without revealing the contractor's name or the details of the dispute.

Don't use closed meetings to discuss unpopular subjects or to avoid confrontation. A board may see an executive session as a closed meeting, but homeowners may see them as secret meetings. Avoid that perception by limiting the number of executive sessions held, announcing them in advance, and explaining why they're being conducted.

Annual Meetings

Your governing documents probably require you to conduct an annual membership meeting during which you present the new budget, elect a board of directors, and hear committee reports. Your documents and state statute specify when and how you are to notify residents of this meeting.

This will be the only meeting many residents attend during the year, so take advantage of the opportunity to communicate with them. Follow the meeting with a social event at which you provide a buffet, invite a guest speaker, or ask homeowners to talk briefly on topics of interest to the community. Circulate among residents and listen to what they have to say during these events.

The election is a very important part of the annual meeting, but you will have to prepare and organize the election well in advance of the meeting date. Your governing documents will specify the particulars of eligibility, the process for obtaining nominations, and other requirements. Consider establishing a nominating committee to oversee and conduct this important function in your association.

Special Meetings

Special meetings are similar to annual meetings with regard to notification, quorum, and other requirements, but they are limited to the particular item of concern or interest for which they were called. They offer an excellent opportunity for a board to present sensitive or controversial matters to residents and to hear what they think.

Town Meetings and Open Forums

Town meetings and open forums provide a structured venue in which groups can explore issues and express opinions. They are business-like events, generally limited to one issue. Town meetings allow you to present a controversial issue to residents and get their feedback before you take action. You can also garner support for large projects or clarify unpopular decisions. If possible, solicit questions from residents before the meeting, then prepare a handout with the answers and distribute it at the meeting.

A town meeting usually has a moderator and some basic rules of conduct, and its objective is to reach consensus, resolve an issue, or answer a question—although not necessarily on the spot.

An open forum is slightly less structured than a town meeting and simply gives everyone an opportunity to voice opinions and share concerns with neighbors. Maybe the county has rezoned the tract adjacent to the association, and residents are unhappy about it. There's not a whole lot that can be done, but scheduling a meeting room for two hours and providing a microphone and a sign-up sheet will help residents work through their anxieties.

Although an open forum doesn't necessarily call for action or resolution from the association, pay attention to what resident have to say. You'll get valuable insights into the character and values of the community.

Informal Meetings

Try conducting informal meetings in a relaxed setting like a coffee hour or an open house. Some people are more comfortable in a smaller, casual gathering and more likely to share their thoughts with board members.

Providing Notice

Providing notice of some meetings, especially the annual meeting, is required by law. Your governing documents or state regulations may specify the means or timing of these notices; and, in some states, "sunshine" laws have placed specific requirements on how and when you should announce meetings.

Keep your notices brief, focused, and simple. Issue them at the appropriate time either by mailing, hand delivering, or posting in a public place. Meeting notices must include the date, time and place, and possibly the agenda or a list of issues being addressed. Ask your association attorney to review your notice and meeting procedures to make sure you're operating correctly, and always have the attorney review your official notices before distributing.

◆ ◆ ◆ ◆

Whatever the setting, any time you're meeting with residents, be prepared to answer tough questions, know your CC&Rs, and make yourself accessible.

Related Resources

Guide to Annual Meetings, Special Meetings & Elections, 3rd Ed., (GAP Report #21). P. Michael Nagle, Community Associations Institute, 1999.
> This report is useful as a play book for self managers to organize and execute the annual meeting. The sections on elections and voting answer a number of questions about quorums, proxies, counting votes, and other details that tend to be forgotten from one year to the next. It also provides information about voting procedures, proxies, and nominating committees. The sample election policy and procedures resolution in the back is a handy off-the-shelf document for establishing your own system.

Conducting Meetings: A Guide to Running Productive Community Association Board Meetings. M.J. Keatts, Ed., Community Associations Institute, 1998.
> This book addresses some of the practical realities of getting people together for a meeting faced by self managers—such as finding a suitable place to meet or deciding whether to video tape or audio tape a meeting. Advice on conducting executive sessions and handling disruptions is presented with perspective and wisdom.

The Art of Successful Meetings. W.D. Southworth, McGraw-Hill, 2000.
> A comprehensive blueprint for self managers on how to chair a meeting and handle motions. Also includes information on voting procedures, quorums, unruly members, nominations, and committees.

Guide for the Presiding Officer: A Functional Guide for Presidents and Chairmen, 2nd Ed., Joyce L. Stephens, Frederick Publishers, 1996.
> This guide presents detailed information on chairing meetings, handling conflict, and communicating effectively.

Chapter 7

Maintenance

One of your important duties, as a self-managing board, is to preserve, protect and enhance the value of your association. The best way to do that is to develop and implement a property maintenance program.

Define Maintenance Responsibility

If you don't already have a comprehensive list of the various physical components of your association, conduct an inventory so that you know exactly what needs to be included in your maintenance plan. Don't be deterred by the magnitude of this task; it's a critical, and often overlooked, step. If you already have an inventory, review it carefully to ensure that it's up to date.

When you've completed the inventory, determine whether the association or the individual homeowner is obligated to maintain each item on the list. Your governing documents should provide the necessary guidance. If they don't, you'll need to adopt policies that do. When you add information about who's responsible for what to the inventory, the result is a maintenance responsibilities chart. This is a useful reference document that you can adopt by resolution and share with the homeowners.

At this stage of planning, don't worry about life expectancies or the conditions of the items listed on your inventory. Those questions will be answered later in a reserve study analysis. Remember that, at this stage, your goal is simply to delineate areas of maintenance responsibility between the association and the individual homeowners.

Why Use a Maintenance Schedule?

- It eliminates unexpected replacements and breakdowns.
- It keeps costs down because repairs are not made on an emergency basis.
- It extends the lives of expensive common elements and reduces reserve funds
- It keeps your stress level down and the residents satisfaction levels up because it stops problems before they occur

Routine and Preventative Maintenance

After getting expert advice from a qualified engineer, you should develop a maintenance schedule for inspecting and repairing your common elements on a regular basis. Monitoring the condition of your property regularly eliminates surprises and helps control costs by reducing unexpected replacements or breakdowns. Inspections and preventative maintenance, as laid out in your maintenance schedule, will extend the life of the common elements significantly. This will reduce the amount of money you must reserve over time by extending the lives of the components covered by your reserves.

Level of Maintenance

You determine the scope of work, or how much maintenance you need, by answering the basic questions: who, what, when, where, and how? Of course, your answers will depend to some degree on what your governing documents allow, what the homeowners expect, and what your budget can afford.

Once you have an idea of the level of maintenance your association needs, create an RFP, and seek the services of qualified service providers to carry out that maintenance for you. Be sure to sign contracts with all service providers specifying the scope of work.

Points to Include in an RFP or Contract

Parties to the Contract: Specify the exact manner in which the contract will be drawn. Include the address of the association, phone numbers, e-mail addresses, and complete names of those who will be the contact for the association. Make sure that the association is the contracting party so that the representatives of the association won't be held personally responsible.

Time Period: Specify the deadline to receive bids, when the work should start, and when you expect it to be completed. The completion date is important since an open-ended contract could drag on for months.

Penalties: Specify penalties for delays, failure to complete work on time, or failure to comply with contract provisions. This will help you prevent problems and provide solutions if you do encounter them.

Payment Schedule and Terms: Specify whether your association will pay by check or cash, on a weekly draw or as work is completed. These terms help you and the contractor avoid confusion and prevent work from stopping during disputes. Also, clarify the invoice procedures: who receives them

Getting Help With an RFP

- The local CAI chapter and other professional groups can sometimes provide assistance.
- Homeowners or board members may have experience or expertise in writing RFPs.
- Architects, engineers, and builders can provide information about the scope of work.
- The public library or web sites may provide valuable background information.
- Contractors can help you determine the scope of work and prepare the specifications. (These contractors should not be allowed to bid on the job, however.)
- Supply firms and manufacturers can help you find qualified contractors to bid on your RFP.
- Other community associations may have experience or documents they can share.

and who approves them. For best results, tie your payments to a specific schedule for completing the work.

Materials: Specify who provides materials and state the quality, type, color, quantity, and delivery means. It should also indicate who is responsible for storing the materials and what will be done with leftovers.

Storage: Make sure you indicate where materials will be stored and who is responsible for security and missing materials.

Damage: Clarify who is responsible for damage to property or injury to people. Specify how damage claims will be handled and who will compensate losses.

Insurance: Talk to your association insurance carrier and decide how much insurance is appropriate and who should provide it. List this in your RFP and contract.

Bonds: Decide whether you think the contractor should be required to put up a bond, including a payment of performance bond.

Guarantee/Warranty: Clearly define the time frame in which warranty work will be performed and by whom.

Clean Up: Require the contractor to clean up the work site, dispose of trash, and police the work area daily. Specify who will provide trash containers, where they will be placed, and how often they will be emptied. Also specify that the contractor must maintain and store tools and equipment in an orderly and safe manner.

On-Site Supervision: Specify that the contractor is to provide on-site supervision of work crews at all times.

Materials Selection: Specify who is responsible for selecting materials and the time frame in which they must be selected.

Progress Inspections: Include a schedule for periodic inspections. These inspections ensure that work is getting done on time and that it complies with the contract specifications. Schedule your inspections at the completion of each stage of work, and ensure that each stage is completed to your satisfaction before allowing work to begin on the next phase.

Notification of Overruns: You should require the contractor to notify the association if it encounters more work than the contract specifies. You should also require that the association must approve the overruns before the additional work is done, and before the additional expense is incurred.

Hold-Back (or Retention): Specify how much of the total payment (usually 10%) will be held back until all work is completed and accepted.

Cancellation: Specify that you will include a 30-day cancellation clause in your contract for on-going service of a general nature.

Compliance with Law: Include a clause that all parties must meet all applicable local, state, and federal laws.

Verbal Agreements: Your contract should specify that it represents the entire understanding between the association and the contractor, and that no verbal agreements have been made or will be honored unless added as a written addendum to the contract.

Location: Specify the exact location of the work to be performed, including address, building numbers, description, and location. If possible, include a map.

Working Hours: Specify what days and hours of the day work may be performed. Provide for make up days, extending hours, and approving changes in the working times.

Scheduled Maintenance

In addition to the routine and ongoing maintenance responsibilities that you take care of, you also have to focus on your long-term maintenance needs. Long-term maintenance schedules are complex and require careful attention to life expectancies and future funding needs. This type of scheduled maintenance should be covered in your reserve plans and funds.

Reserve funds are set aside to replace major components of an association's property such as the roof. The funds are set aside over time not only so that they are available when the item deteriorates, but also to equalize the contributions of old and new owners alike.

Unscheduled Maintenance

Occasionally, your property will need restoration or upgrading. You should

Why Do You Need Reserve Funds?

- The secondary mortgage market requires your association to have reserve funds. Fannie Mae, Freddie Mac, FHA, and VA may not mortgage units in your association if you do not meet the legal, fiduciary and professional requirements of these lenders.

- Your state statutes, regulations, or case law require your association to have reserve funds.

- Your association governing documents require your association to have reserve funds.

- Accounting standards require your association to have reserve funds.

- Reserve funds are fair to all residents. Although a roof will be only be replaced about every 25 years, every owner who lived under it during those 25 years should contribute to its replacement cost.

- Reserve funds minimize or eliminate the need for special assessments.

- Reserve funds enhance sales. Your state may require you to disclose the amounts in your reserve funds to prospective buyers. Well-funded reserve accounts tell buyers your association is financially sound.

employ a qualified engineer to advise you on services and materials. When you're budgeting for restorations or new facilities, consider not only the initial cost, but also pay particular attention to the long-term impact on future budgets. Skimping now on materials to save money may cost more over the years for maintenance or replacement. Make sure your engineer understands your budgetary requirements.

◆◆◆◆

Although only one star in the constellation of association issues, maintenance is the one that shines the brightest and gets the most attention from residents. If the community doesn't sparkle, a self manager will hear about it immediately. Use a good maintenance plan to keep your association in top condition, to keep curb appeal high, and to keep your property values where they belong.

Related Resources

Grounds Maintenance for the Community Association, 2nd Ed., (GAP Report #11). Bette A. Weseman, PCAM® Community Associations Institute, 1998.

> Although not specifically addressed in *Self-Management*, grounds maintenance is an important aspect of managing associations with large common areas. While you'll likely employ professionals to service the grounds, you'll still want a good understanding of maintenance practices, and you'll need to develop a maintenance plan. This plan is needed for budgeting purposes, it provides the basis for an RFP for selecting a contractor, and it amounts to a work plan for the grounds crew to implement. GAP 11 takes the self-managing board through this process step by step.

Selecting the Landscape Maintenance Contractor, James B. Cranford, AMS®, PCAM® (GAP Report #12). Community Associations Institute, 1996.

> A companion and logical follow on to GAP 11, this report gets into more detail on finding the right service provider and working successfully with them. Self managers who are aware of environmental issues will find both these reports sensitive to their concerns.

Bid Specifications & Contract Preparation, 3rd Ed., (GAP Report #9). Stephen R. Bupp, CMCA®, AMS®, PCAM®, Community Associations Institute, 1997.

> For detailed instruction and advice on bidding and contracting, self managers should refer to this report. Information on what to expect when working with contractors will be especially helpful to those who are new to the process.

A Complete Guide to Reserve Funding and Reserve Investment Strategies, 5th Ed., (GAP Report #24). Frumkin & Juall, Eds., Community Associations Institute, 2001.

> The importance of maintaining adequate reserves can't be overstated. This chapter only touches on the subject, but it deserves thorough study by self managers. GAP 24 provides the in-depth information that is beyond the reach of *Self-Management*, self managers will find it an invaluable component in their community association education.

Chapter 8

Communication

Communication is a dynamic process, perhaps nowhere more so than in a community association, where it encompasses publications, resident interaction, Web sites, public relations, being in touch with the larger community, and even public affairs. All of these work together to complement and bolster one another.

In order for you to be a successful board member and manager, communication must be two-way. That means you must take advantage of and even create venues that make you available to residents. Meetings are a natural way to do this, and the chapter on meetings provides more information on the several types and purposes of meetings.

From a communications perspective, the important thing when meeting with residents—whether in a casual one-on-one conversation or at the annual meeting—is to be accessible and prepared to answer tough questions. Make sure you know your CC&Rs and that you're well informed on all association matters. Also, be willing to really listen to and seriously consider what residents are saying.

Surveys

Beyond face-to-face meetings, you can glean valuable information from your residents through surveys. Learn how residents want their money spent by asking them. This will help you establish standards consistent with the wishes of the majority.

Make it easy to use. To get the right information, a survey must be easy to read and easy to answer. Open-ended questions can elicit all kinds of answers, so focus the responses by asking questions that can be answered "Strongly Agree," "Somewhat Agree," "Somewhat Disagree," and "Strongly Disagree."

Don't be too specific. Ask questions that focus on the big picture. For example, ask if the association should build a clubhouse, not whether it should be painted green.

Be concise. Keep your surveys short—no more than one or two pages. The longer it is, the more intimidating it is. Put short surveys in your newsletter and perhaps reach a larger or more motivated audience. This also saves on printing and mailing costs.

Pace yourself. Don't overdo it. One or two surveys a year will keep owners from feeling bombarded and keep the format effective.

Share the results. Publish survey findings in your newsletter and on your Web site so residents know if their thoughts are similar to their neighbors. If you make a decision based on the survey, let everyone know that, too. People like to know that completing a survey means something, and that someone actually considered their opinion.

Community Association Publications

There are several types of communications resources your association can publish. Heading the list is your newsletter.

Newsletters

Whether you're revamping or introducing your association's newsletter, think about what you want to include. What's been left out of the old newsletter, or

---

Communications Basics

Few efforts will contribute more to the success of a self-managing board and to the harmony of the community than good communications. A few basic guidelines that contribute to effective communications include:

- Communicate frequently. Don't be afraid to deliver important messages repeatedly.
- Communicate in varying settings and places—some formal, some informal.
- Communicate in as many ways as possible. Publish a newsletter, hold a town meeting, create a Web site, or host a social event.
- Be positive, open, and direct. Provide as much information as possible, and don't withhold information.
- Listen. Communication is a two-way process. Get input from residents and seriously consider what they have to say.
- Be inclusive. Remember that your association may include tenants, people with disabilities, older persons, non-English-speaking residents, families and singles, and others.
- Be professional. You represent many others each time you communicate.
- Identify your goal: What do you want to accomplish?
- Consider the urgency of your message. How quickly do residents need to receive this information?
- Know your audience. For whom is your message intended?
- Decide what you want to spend. What is an appropriate expense for delivering this message?
- Use the right tone: What type of presentation is appropriate to achieve your goal?

---

what do you want to accomplish with this brand-new newsletter?

Categorizing information in your newsletter by departments gives you a way to regularly remind residents of rules, call attention to events, and report association activities. Some suggested departments:

Personnel Notes: Identify and thank volunteers, acknowledge promotions, and recognize accomplishments—in and outside the association.

Message From the Board: Ask a different board member to write a message for each issue. Make sure all of their names appear in every issue.

Contact Corner: Print the names, addresses, and phone numbers of people the residents should contact for maintenance or repairs, emergencies, or announcements.

Committee Reports: Keep residents informed of what's going on and aware of the work being done by the association's committees. Ask committee members to write articles on their activities if reports aren't available.

Rule Reminder: Is the poop getting scooped? Are residents adhering to parking rules? Rules that are violated repeatedly can be highlighted and, perhaps more importantly, explained in a regular department.

Events: When there's a pool party or a seminar on safety, let everyone know by keeping a two-to three-month event calendar in the same place on the same page of every issue.

Keep your newsletter vibrant and thriving by putting these additional tips into practice:

Put some zing in your headlines. Draw attention to the information you're supplying by putting a good headline on it. "Annual Meeting Held" will not get as much attention as "Board Announces Plan to Raise Assessments." Puns, rhymes, wordplay on titles of books, movies, and TV shows also will pull readers into an article. Be creative.

Give all of the facts. Every story should include the basic who, what, why, where, when, and how. Never assume your readers know what you're talking about.

Make articles easy to scan. Newsletter articles should be short and easy to read. People are flooded with information and they don't have time to read heavily detailed articles. This may seem at odds with "Give all of the facts," but detailed, contextual information actually will make an article that much easier for busy people to read.

Don't bury information. Important information should come at the beginning of an article, not at the end.

Proofread. Typographical errors are unavoidable, but too many will destroy your credibility. Different people catch different types of errors so each issue should be looked at by at least two people. Always check the spellings of residents' names. Also, check corrections—sometimes a new error is inadvertently introduced when correcting an old one.

Be on the lookout for story ideas. You want to keep residents up to date on association business, but you also want to publicize the contributions of volunteers and promote association events. Consider different ways of presenting information as well. A question-and-answer format might help you explain an assessment hike.

Share good news. From winning awards to taking on new projects, a newsletter can help you promote the association and its accomplishments.

Be consistent in your design. Develop a template and stick with it. This blueprint helps set the newsletter apart from other information your residents receive. Also, when they recognize the newsletter, they're more likely to pick it up and read it.

Don't be afraid of white space. To avoid a cluttered look, allow a margin of three-quarters of an inch around the edge of the page. Allow a quarter-to half-inch between columns. A clean look organizes the page, frames the text, and gives everything breathing room.

Include photographs and art. Make sure you write captions that complement the art. But don't feel that every inch of space must be cluttered. A good piece of art draws the reader in and emphasizes your point. It should never detract from the article.

Distribute regularly to all owners and residents. Deliver the newsletter at the same time every month or every other month. You want residents to rely on the newsletter; if they receive it inconsistently, it becomes just another piece of junk mail.

One last recommendation about newsletters: Consider adopting a newsletter policy for your association—particularly if you delegate newsletter production to volunteers. A newsletter policy provides a useful framework within which everyone can work comfortably to produce your newsletter. It should specify what content is acceptable, who decides what gets published in each issue, what types of information get priority, the minimum level of verification required before a story will be published, the need to adhere to the association's governing documents and avoid libel, what types of advertisements, if any, are acceptable to the association, and the ceiling for ad revenue according to your tax status.

10 Ways to Communicate with Residents

1. Hold town meetings on special topics (e.g., parking, facilities, amenities).
2. Have social events at which neighbors can interact with board members.
3. Respond quickly to resident inquiries. Respond to phone calls within 12 hours and to written inquiries within a week.
4. Encourage residents to observe board meetings and allow time for questions.
5. Publish meeting minutes.
6. Put divisive issues to a vote.
7. Encourage residents to form advisory committees.
8. Put a positive spin on newsletter stories, promoting your association's accomplishments whenever possible.
9. Create a youth board. Let teenagers give you insight into what can help your association serve your community.
10. Publish and distribute an annual report.

Annual Reports

Let people know what you've accomplished (and what to look forward to) in an annual report. Residents will appreciate that you're keeping them apprised of the past and involved in the future. An annual report is a concise and permanent record of your association's accomplishments, an effective marketing piece with realtors, and a valuable resource for new residents.

Include a review of your key accomplishments, but don't list routine tasks. Provide an overview of the association's finances, and include the budget for the coming year. List the names of all volunteers—regardless of the extent of their efforts—who worked for the association during the year. Provide statistics, when you can, such as the number of homes in your association sold during the year and their high and low selling prices or the ratio of owner-occupied to leased units in your association. Also provide a glimpse of the coming year in your annual report. Remember to present your information positively and to keep it in perspective.

Resident Handbooks

A resident handbook can be a useful general reference for all residents. It should reference the association's governing documents, describe their importance, and summarize their purpose and content. A resident handbook should also include a copy of the association rules. Other components might include a directory of key contacts, association statistics like size and age, copies of forms commonly needed by residents, financial information like the budget and insurance requirements, and answers to common questions like "How do I register my car?" Providing information in a resident handbook not only helps residents, it helps you by cutting down on calls.

Information Technology

The more your association can use information technology the easier it will be for you to govern *and* manage. For example, an online presence improves not only communication but also legal and financial transactions. Members can pay assessments, check the status of their accounts, report problems, review governing documents, post notices to the electronic bulletin board, read newsletters or meeting minutes, participate in surveys, and even cast votes online.

Web Sites

As a medium, the Web is well suited for disseminating community association information like CC&Rs, newsletters, news updates, or upcoming events. Unlike a monthly publication or a special flier, a Web site can do this continuously, and it can be reached by residents who are away for extended periods. It's doubtful that paper will ever be replaced completely, but compared to print publications, a Web site gives you more bang for the buck. And you can go one step further and offer flash e-mailing of breaking news to anyone who signs up for it.

Valuable as they are, publications like your newsletter have their limits. Timeliness and affordability are two of them. You can post information on your association's Web site cheaper and faster than you can publish it any other way. Creating a Web site can be as complex or simple an exercise as you want it to be.

You can hire professional help, do it yourself, or try some combination of the two.

Many service providers specialize in creating and maintaining Web sites specifically for community associations. The cost depends on the size of the site and the features involved, but these companies generally understand what their clients want: to strengthen the lines of communication with their residents. Typically, after launching a Web site, a company will key in any updates or new material that its client association sends in a few times a month.

Doing it yourself is probably the most economical solution, but it leaves the association relying almost solely on the technical expertise and the commitment level of a volunteer. You could have problems when the volunteer moves or simply gets tired of putting in all that unpaid work. While this option isn't for everybody, it probably isn't as hard as you think.

If you decide to do it yourself, get one of the many books available that teach HTML—the programming language that creates web pages. You can also purchase software that will help you learn HTML and establish your web presence. In just a few days, you'll see that it's pretty easy to make a simple Web site by starting with text documents you already have. The only other thing you'll need is an image or two.

For images, you'll need either to find electronic images you like (look through photo and clip-art libraries on CD-ROM), or to put in your own photos using a scanner and your choice of photo-editing software. A trip to your local computer store should get you everything you need. Most new scanners come with the software you need and offer instructions for making Web-ready images.

Once you have your Web pages and associated images, you're ready to put your site on the Internet. Find a good local hosting company by asking friends and colleagues who have Web sites, or look through the business classified ads in your local paper or phone book. Your hosting company can provide space on an Internet-connected computer and set up your domain name—the name of your site, like www.caionline.org. Your hosting company can also help you with all the details of uploading your site.

Some vendors will set up your association's Web site at no charge, then turn the reins over to a resident to serve as administrator. The association then pays a monthly fee to the company to host the site (and possibly to provide ongoing assistance). Procedures usually are kept simple—typically, the designated administrator needs only a Web browser to add announcements, documents, links, and whatever else to the site.

Once your site is uploaded and available for the world to see, tell people about it, and include the address on all of your correspondence so visitors can see the result of your efforts.

Use your Web sit to market your association, and put your best face forward. Some associations use their sites entirely for marketing, with photos and information on specific units for sale.

Create an archive in which you place past association newsletters, meeting minutes, budgets, and annual reports, and other documents. It can save a lot of time when you need to track down dated information, and it gives residents a sense of the history and character of the community.

Use online polls to survey your residents—they're a quick, tidy way to sample public opinion. How do your residents feel about putting in speed bumps? Is there any interest in an association-wide pool party? These aren't binding referendums—but there is the potential for Internet voting.

Give residents the opportunity to get to know one another with association message boards and chat rooms. Some association sites offer resident profiles—names, birthdays, occupations, interests—as well as movie, restaurant, or book reviews.

Take advantage of your Web site to cut down on management processes. Post your forms online and allow residents to submit them electronically, and, if your budget can bear it, provide account information like balances or interest accrual to residents on your Web site.

The Web is a flexible medium, meaning in some ways you're limited only by your imagination.

E-mail

E-mail provides an easy means to communicate for board members, service providers, residents, and virtually anyone who has a modem and an e-mail address. It's almost too convenient; you can read your e-mail whenever and usually wherever you want without playing phone tag or being interrupted, and it also provides a written record.

Be sure to apply to your e-mail communications the same common sense you use with other types of communication. For example, instructions exchanged by e-mail with a vendor regarding a particular project should be coordinated through one contact person. Otherwise, the vendor may have to deal with conflicting or overlapping information from several people.

In addition to sending quick communications, you can also send files such as minutes or newsletter articles. This gives everyone a quick review of drafts, reduces postage costs, and gets the document finalized in less time.

List Serves

List serves are a convenient and economical way to disseminate information among a large number of people. Information is delivered in e-mail format to subscribers who can then respond to all other subscribers with comments of their own. In this way, a list serve uniquely promotes association-to-member and member-to-member communication. Associations can use a list serve to deliver newsletters to residents who prefer the electronic edition to paper.

Intranets

An Intranet site is similar to a Web site, but access is restricted to subscribers. The advantage over a Web site is that subscribers can post information on the Intranet site, and certain activities, such as your last site log on, can be recorded. In order to subscribe, a person must first have log-on and password information. In this way, you can restrict Intranet use to association members or residents, for example.

Intranet sites offer a hybrid of Web site and e-mail benefits. They allow board members to post information in one place for everyone to access. If the board needs to review the latest version of the architect's plans for the new clubhouse before the next meeting, the drawings can't be shared through e-mail. However, they can be posted to the Intranet site (possibly by the architect, if you supply the password), and board members can record their comments for everyone to read prior to the meeting.

Media Relations

The stereotype of the overbearing community association has—unfortunately—become ingrained in the national consciousness because of a few hysterically publicized stories. Even more unfortunate, it too often informs the actions of the reporters and producers dispatched to cover the next Big Story. If that story happens in your association, be prepared to make your side of the story known, and follow these tips when working with the media:

- Be honest, or be as honest as the demands of privacy and confidentiality will allow you. Anything less than the truth will only come back to haunt you.
- Designate a spokesperson. It helps if you refer all media inquiries to one person, be it your board president, attorney, or a special public relations officer.
- Assume you're speaking on the record. If you don't want to be quoted, you must specifically tell a reporter that your comments are not for publication. Otherwise, assume they are.
- Get the facts straight. If you're unsure of what has happened, is happening, or will happen, don't be afraid to tell the reporter that you're not prepared at that moment but that you'll check and call him or her back later.
- Don't repeat a negative statement. Sound-bite-worthy phrases have a way of insinuating themselves into a controversy, then getting repeated so often they become a story's quasi-official, accepted phrase—thus, your association has "banned street play." To counter this journalistic shorthand, try to rephrase any negative questions to sound positive. Q: "Why has your association banned street play?" A: "Why have we designated several spots away from the street for children to play? It's a safety issue. We want our kids to be able to run around without any chance of getting hit by a car."
- Don't call people names. Tempting as it might be, it does absolutely no good. You'll only sound unprofessional, defensive, and—just like the stereotype says—overbearing. Stick to the facts of the case, and leave the editorializing to someone else.

- Maintain your composure. Don't antagonize reporters. The good ones are only doing their job and are genuinely interested in getting every side of a story. And if you fly off the handle, you risk souring the relationship with someone who can make things more difficult than they have to be.

- Be gracious. Your first response to a media call should never be, "There's no story! I don't know why you're wasting your time on this!" There's no better way to convince a reporter that in fact there is a story—and that you're hiding something.

- Be brief. If you have a chance, give some thought to what you might say before you talk to a reporter. Clearly state why your association took the action it did.

- Don't use the terms "us" and "them." This only reinforces the holier-than-thou stereotype of community association boards. Instead, refer to specific people and specific institutions by name. Homeowners should always be "Ms. Smith" or "Mr. Jones," and the board should be "the Sleepy Valley Homeowner Association" or, if need be, "the board." And remember to stress that any homeowner can serve on the board.

- Be proactive. Believe it or not, newspapers and TV stations do like good news. If your association has done something you think is newsworthy—a charity car wash, a holiday festival, an enlightened revision of your governing documents—consider contacting the media yourself. See if they're interested in a positive development.

The Local Community

Your community association isn't a discrete or isolated entity, it's an integral part of the larger community, and communicating with people and groups around you will make self management a little easier.

Civic organizations, local businesses, realtors, and other community associations are the groups you're most likely to encounter because they're interwoven with the fabric of your association.

If service organizations like Rotary Club or Lions are strong in your area, canvas your association to see if any residents are club members—they can be helpful liaisons to the local chapter. Also, if they're active in service organizations, they might be good candidates for committee slots or board nominations.

Even if you don't have an "in," consider approaching these organizations—particularly when you need a little extra help. These activities benefit your association because they bring community members together and foster positive neighbor interactions.

The same holds true for local businesses. Let merchants know of the buying power of your members. Encourage them to support community events by donating door prizes, for example. In return, make a commitment to support them when you need a caterer for the annual meeting or when you need to rent equipment.

Reaching out to the real-estate industry in your area and establishing a comfortable relationship with key agents will increase sales and benefit your association in a number of ways. Your buildings may be 20 years older than the new homes just built across the street, but do the local realtors know that your reserves are fully funded and that gas and water are included in the monthly assessment? That information can quickly offset curb appeal.

Put an "Information for Realtors" page on your Web site. If you don't have a Web page, draft a one-page flier with a bulleted list of selling features for your association. Realtors will appreciate knowing some of these details about your community because it makes their jobs easier. The association benefits because successful sales minimize rentals, and generally stimulate the economy in your area.

Establish a dialog with the other community associations in your area, especially if you share common interests. If the phone company wants to erect a 200-foot relay tower between your association and the community adjacent to you, negotiating the exact location of the tower with the phone company will be easier and the outcome better if two associations work together.

Communicating With Government Officials

Chapter 11 on public policy provides compelling arguments for getting involved in public affairs and some practical information on how to go about it. When the time actually comes to communicate with government officials, there are several approaches you can take.

A letter is one of the best means for communicating with government officials because it creates a record of your position. Make sure it's legible—either printed or typed—and that it's addressed correctly. Keep your letter to about one page, and send it while the issue is current or before a vote has been taken. Always be polite and positive, never critical or threatening. If you've had previous contact with this official, mention the date or event. Let the official know something about your association—particularly how many constituents are in it—and state whether you're speaking for the entire association.

State the purpose of your letter, and cite specific numbers and names of pending legislation if appropriate. In your own words explain how this issue

---

Basic Guidelines for Communicating With Government Officials

- Be prepared. Make sure you're familiar with the issue and know the exact bill name or number.
- Identify yourself as a constituent, and indicate that you represent a community association.
- Describe your association size in voters, not units.
- State your position briefly and positively.
- Be specific about what you want to happen and why it's important.
- Be courteous, and don't argue—just state your position.
- Follow up on everything. Follow a phone call or visit with a letter or e-mail. Follow a letter with a phone call. This is an opportunity to reiterate your position.

will affect your association, and specify what action you'd like the official to take. Be sure to thank the official for his or her attention to your concerns, and ask for a response.

When time is short, you can fax or e-mail your letter. Call the official's office and find out which staff member is handling the issue. Fax your letter using a cover sheet to that person or put that person's name in the subject field of your e-mail.

You can also phone public officials, but don't expect to talk directly to the official. A staff member will likely take a detailed message and pass it along. Be prepared with all the information listed above.

Unlike other forms of communication, a personal visit gives you an opportunity to educate officials and their staff, to provide them with background materials, and to show them first hand how committed and concerned you are. To arrange a visit, call the official's office and ask to schedule an appointment. Prepare a written statement of your position to provide at the meeting, and agree ahead of time who will speak for your group. Follow up with a personal thank-you note or letter; and restate your position and summarize your understanding of what will be done next. Stay in touch with the official or staff member, and develop the relationship with ongoing correspondence and future visits.

◆ ◆ ◆ ◆

Don't assume that communication in your community is somehow just taking place by itself, or that everyone knows what you know or shares your opinion. Dispel this illusion by developing and implementing a cohesive communications program. Nothing will contribute more to productive meetings, satisfied homeowners, balanced budgets, informed consultants, supportive residents, cooperative tenants, eager buyers, and low delinquencies as strong communications. It doesn't take as much effort as you might think, and the return on your investment will be well worth it.

Related Resource

Communications for Community Associations, 4th Ed., (GAP Report #15). Debra H. Lewin, Community Associations Institute, 2000.

Good communication is probably the leading indicator of success in community associations, and self managers are encouraged to make every effort to educate themselves on its many facets. Countless books have been written on newsletter production, media and government relations, letter writing, conducting meetings, and the other vehicles discussed in this chapter—all of which are useful. Similarly, GAP 15 gets into greater detail on many of these topics, but it presents practical information from within the peculiar paradigm of the community association.

Chapter 9

Financial Management

One of the most important business functions of a self-managing board is managing the association's finances. This responsibility rests with the board, but there's plenty of help available for various tasks from qualified professionals.

You don't need to be an expert in finances, but you should be able to establish prudent financial policies and procedures. Weigh the advice you get from the professionals against your best judgment and the desires of the members, and then make sound decisions based on your knowledge of the association.

There are numerous areas of financial responsibility where you, as a managing board, must stay active and remain informed.

Financial Policies

All associations, and especially the self managed, need to establish and follow a few fundamental financial policies. These provide a framework within which to work and add a layer of protection for the association in general and the self-managing board in particular.

Investment Policy

As a board, you'll decide how to invest the association's funds—usually the reserves. An investment policy provides continuity from present to subsequent members of the board and ensures that association funds are managed consistently from one board to the next. Another big advantage is that it protects the association from well-meaning board members who may have differing approaches to risk taking.

Protecting the principle should be the core of an association's investment policy. A policy requiring that all association funds be placed in government-insured accounts or similarly protected investments would be appropriate. In fact, this strategy may be required by your governing documents, therefore, as with all policy making, check your documents first to ensure your policies are in line.

Your investment policy should also state that accounts will not exceed the amount insured, and that your association will only engage the services of insured, licensed, and bonded agents.

Collections Policy

A written collections policy is a must for any association. It should be given to all new association members and distributed from time to time to all owners as a reminder. This policy should outline the association's authority to collect assessments, state in a positive way why assessments are important, and perhaps list the services that they cover. The policy should state the consequences of failing to pay assessments and the steps the association will take to enforce the policy.

Signature Policy

Your financial policies should include guidance on who can sign for the association and what transactions require signature. For example, your policy might require two signatures for expenditures over a certain amount or it may state that funds can only be moved by signature, not by phone. Be sure your policy also covers who can sign for transactions such as fund transfers.

Budgets

You'll project your association's operations for the upcoming year using a budget. Prepare it well in advance so that you can get an idea of how much you need to assess the members. Your budget is essential for projecting the type, quality, timing and continuity of the services your members will need. Prepare it carefully and use it as a planning tool.

Your state may regulate how you prepare your budget. Ask your attorney to review state stature to make sure you comply. Also, check with your association's CPA for guidance in preparing your budget

Budgets identify projected income and expenses for two basic functional areas: operations and reserves. Budget significant and distinct operations and activities separately. The income side of a budget typically lists revenues from assessments, investment income, fees and penalties, and miscellaneous or other income. Expenses tend to be grouped in categories like maintenance, insurance, utilities, professional fees, taxes, and so on.

Operating budgets reflect the association's anticipated daily and ongoing operations. List them in the budget in logical groups according to how you manage and account for the activities. List these groups in your accounting records in a similar fashion in order to account for the transactions as they occur.

Your reserve budget should reflect the association's current year funding obligations for the long-term repair or replacement of common property. Expenditures relating to reserve items need to be considered, but only to the extent that the expenditure will exceed funds set aside for that purpose. If you expect expenses to exceed the funds available, consider alternate sources of funds. This can include special assessments, delaying the expenditure until funds are available, borrowing from other reserve or operating funds (if allowed by law) or borrowing from a bank.

Your budget will help you set your annual assessments. For example, if you borrowed money and have to make loan payments, you need to include this in your budget and consider it in setting assessments. On the other hand, if your association depreciates these assets, the depreciation may appear on a budget but would not be used to set assessments.

Budget Building

There are a few basic steps to follow as you develop your budget.

- Check your governing documents and board minutes to ensure that you're familiar with all your obligations. Governing documents may require that certain conditions be met. Past minutes will remind you that the board voted for a new pool cover last fall and you need to budget for it.
- Review the past year's financial statements and compare them to last year's budget. Adjust those line items that vary significantly.
- Find out what things will cost in the coming year. If you don't have all your service contracts signed prior to developing the budget, call your current service providers and ask them if they anticipate any rate increases. Call the utility companies and ask them similar questions. They can generally give you estimated percentage increases or decreases that you can apply to your figures. Consult your CPA, investment broker, or bank for estimates on interest earnings; project them conservatively.
- Using last year's budget as a baseline, consider each expense line and decide what should be cut or what needs to be added. Allocations in last year's budget for the new carpet in the lobby can be deleted and the pool cover should be added. Be sure to include projects carried forward from the last budget cycle.

Part of your budgeting process might depend on cash flow. For example, assessments for recreational associations may be paid only annually. Some associations collect assessments only quarterly. Factor these variations into your budgeting. For example, in order to earn the most interest you might sequence your spending throughout the year even if your assessment revenues accrue only once.

The Budget Preparation Schedule

Developing a budget can be a complex activity. A preparation schedule is important because it ensures that the budget is finalized and approved prior to the fiscal year that it covers. In general, the steps in preparing the budget will include:

- Gather whatever financial data you'll need. For example, if you plan a reserve analysis, conduct it prior to the budget cycle so that the results can be incorporated into the budget. Obtain bids for coming year contracts or ask contractors if and how much they may raise their rates in the coming year.

- Create a working draft. Depending on the size of your association, the board may want to form a budget committee to assist in this process.
- Circulate the draft to the association members. Allow members ample opportunity for input and give due consideration to their comments. Your governing documents or state law may specify when the association's budget must be made available to the members or how much time they should be given to review and comment. In any event, be sure to schedule plenty of time for this important notification.
- Revise the draft as needed.
- Present the final budget to the association members and have them vote to approve it. Members may or may not have to approve your association's budget, but they probably do need to approve a dues increase, so if an increase is part of your budget proposal, this step is essential.

Assessments

One of the primary financial activities for any association—and a major fiduciary responsibility for its board—is collecting assessments. Consider-

---

Good Sense Financial Procedures

Ensure that you're using good internal controls for your association by following a few basic procedures.

Cash Transactions
- Keep cash transactions to a minimum.
- Make sure more than one person handles cash transactions.
- Never make a payment in cash. Always write a check.

Processing and Using Checks
- Make all payments by check.
- Never write a check to "cash." Write it to a payee.
- Require two signatures on checks—at least those with large amounts.
- Make sure the person who approves expenditures is not the person writing the checks.
- Don't accept checks made out to a board member. All checks to the association should be payable to the association.
- Secure all checks and deposit them daily.
- Establish a lockbox account with the bank for collecting assessments.

Checks and Balances
- Make sure the person who records transactions is not the person making deposits.

ing the magnitude of this responsibility, it's best to have a collections policy in effect.

Collections Policy

Your collections policy should specify the due date for payments and what happens if payments are late. For example, will you allow a grace period or charge late fees immediately? If you charge late fees, the policy should specify what they are and when they'll be applied. Your policy can give the board a little flexibility to consider special cases, but the policy should also suggest the criteria for special cases and the limits of flexibility.

Make sure all members have copies of the budget and the collections policy. Include them in new member packages and reprint them in your newsletter at least annually.

Collections Process

Once your collections policy is in effect, you face the practical reality of actually collecting the money. You're going to need a workable collections system.

What's workable will depend on your individual circumstances. A small association might use methods that would be unmanageable for a very large association. Similarly the automation that would ease collections for a large community might be too expensive for a small or self-managed association.

In general, the choices include:

- Members personally deliver payments to a central location such as an office.
- Members mail payments to a post office box, an accountant, bookkeeper, treasurer, or bank lockbox.
- Members make arrangements with their banks for automatic fund transfers or preauthorized drafts.
- Members pay by credit card.

In each case, the association will need to set up systems to accommodate whatever method you want to use. For example, if members are allowed to drop off payments, the association will need to send out monthly invoices and ensure that the office is open and staffed at convenient times. If you want members to mail their payments, you'll need to order payment coupons and set up a lockbox account with the bank. Or you may need to set up an account with the bank for processing credit cards.

If you can use a bank lockbox to receive payments, you'll find it has several advantages. It ensures that payments go into the association's account immediately, it saves time for board members or bookkeepers who don't have to process the checks, and it reduces the opportunities for checks to be lost or misdirected.

Payment coupons are also useful because they're convenient, they provide a regular reminder, convey a sense of importance of the payment—similar to the member's mortgage—and they help even out cash flow. If you use coupons, it's a good idea to provide return envelopes as well.

Taxes

Even though your association is a nonprofit organization, you must file a federal, and possibly state and local, income tax return annually—even if you don't owe any taxes. If previous boards failed to file, that doesn't mean you don't have to. In fact, you may need to go back and submit the missing returns.

There are two ways to approach your income taxes. You can file Form 1120H if you meet certain requirements, and you'll be taxed like a homeowners association. Or you can file Form 1120 and be taxed like a regular corporation. Which return your association files can have a big impact on the amount of tax you pay and when you pay it—it also determines your risk in the event of an audit. It's actually an extremely complex question affected by countless variables. The best thing you can do is hire a tax professional well versed in what the IRS calls common-interest realty associations.

How you file your state income tax return will depend on where you live. Again, consult your tax professional for guidance in this area.

Some of your revenues may be subject to sales tax, payroll tax, or property tax depending on the nature of your association and its revenues. If your association runs any type of concession as part of a recreational facility, for example, local sales taxes might be due. Payroll taxes—social security, workers compensation, etc.—will only apply if your association directly employs anyone. This doesn't apply to consultants or contractors, only employees. Property taxes for community associations can be very complex. For example, if not valued correctly, associations may be double taxed. These issues require the expertise of a CPA.

Be sure your association CPA specializes in community association issues to ensure that your association is taxed appropriately and that it complies with all filing requirements.

Audits

Your governing documents, and possibly state statute, may require that your association be audited. If they don't, it's a good idea to have one nevertheless.

The association's CPA is qualified to perform the audit, and he or she will require numerous records. Gathering these will be a simple matter if the association has maintained thorough and well-organized records throughout the year. The CPA may also wish to speak to contractors and others involved with the association to complete the audit.

The CPA will confirm bank balances, conduct inspections, trace transactions, verify payments, and examine numerous other records. The final audit will include the CPA's opinion of the association's financial situation; however, neither the association's financial policies nor the board's use of resources is factored into this opinion.

You should plan to do an audit once a year. If you undergo a change— like assuming control from a developer—an audit is a good idea. Also, there are levels of audits called compilations and reviews that may be appropriate during times of change. As always, check with your accountant.

Keeping Records

State law and your governing documents should specify what financial records your association must maintain. You must maintain them with enough detail to manage the association effectively, and they must track the results of financial transactions.

Accounting software packages are affordable; but, they may not be programmed for certain aspects of association activities. Off-the-shelf business accounting software may not adequately handle such unique needs as maintenance fee receivables, special assessments, or reserve and replacement funds. If you do decide to automate your accounting processes, check with your CPA or other qualified professional before deciding on accounting software to ensure your system is compatible with your accountant's. Also, be sure to have a knowledgeable financial professional set up your accounts in the software and train you how to maintain them.

If your association manages a golf course, dining room, or concession of any type, maintain financial records for them that give you an idea of their profitability. You can't manage these functions effectively unless you know what they're earning and how much they're costing. Be sure your system captures this information.

Reports

You'll want to summarize your finances from time to time in various financial reports. These reports enable you to make informed decisions; they provide a means of conveying information to the members, financial institutions, and vendors; and they fulfill various legal requirements. Review your governing documents, state statutes, and loan documents to find out what reports you may be required to produce. Check with your association attorney or accountant if you're unsure.

Financial statements raise members' comfort levels about how you're using their money. Provide financial statements to your members at regular intervals throughout the year and no less than annually.

Prepare your reports using your accounting software or have your accountant prepare them. Make sure they are accurate and timely. Include a balance sheet and a statement of revenues and expenses in your reports. You may also want to include statements of cash flows and changes in fund balances.

The balance sheet will show your members the financial condition of the association on any particular date. It lists all the property the association owns (assets) and amounts owed by the association to others (liabilities). The difference between assets and liabilities is the association's net worth, or the fund balance. You should show a fund balance for reserves and for operating costs, to get a proper measure of the association's financial condition. Obviously, you want to have more assets than liabilities—or a positive net worth.

The statement of revenues and expenses summarizes the association's operations over a period of time. List your revenues first and subtotal them. Group your expenses in meaningful categories and subtotal them also. Then subtract expenses from revenues to determine the association's net income or loss for that period.

Compare your statement of revenues and expenses for a given period with the budget for that same period to get an idea of how your association is performing. To be effective, your statement of revenues and expenses should also show activities on reserve accounts and special assessments. Be sure to separate these from the operations statement.

The statement of changes in fund balances ties together the balance sheet and the statement of revenues and expenses. The net worth of the association is shown on the balance sheet and is directly impacted by net income or loss.

The statement of cash flow summarizes your association's cash transactions. This statement contains many elements of a statement of revenues and expenses, but it also shows how cash is being used for investing or other financial activities.

Cash or Accrual?

You can account for your association's finances using the cash basis, accrual basis, or something in between called the modified accrual basis.

Cash basis. The cash basis is the easiest method to use, but it won't accurately reflect your association's true financial condition—it simply shows the result of cash transactions. What's missing in the cash method are outstanding assessments and unpaid expenses, and that distorts your financial condition and possibly your decision making. Therefore, you should consider using the accrual method in order to get an accurate picture of your association's financial condition. It's slightly more difficult to prepare and a little more time consuming, but well worth the effort.

Accrual basis. From a practical standpoint, the accrual method of accounting makes the most sense because it's similar to the budget, which is also an accrual document. Accrual basis financial statements are more useful for comparing results of one period to another. With the cash basis you have variances because transactions take place at different times. For instance, if you happen to make a payment at the end of the year and it's a little late, you'd have 11 payments in one year and 13 in the other. With the accrual method, all 12 payments would be in the current year no matter when you paid the bill.

Modified accrual basis. Community associations, being the unique entities that they are, find that a hybrid system called the modified accrual basis works best. Under this system only the large accounts like assessments are maintained using the accrual method. All three methods are appropriate in the right circumstances for interim reports. The modified accrual basis allows the association to gain the most accurate picture of its financial well being.

Other Financial Considerations
Oversight

Implement some type of oversight procedures to keep problems to a minimum. Reconcile bank statements immediately and resolve any discrepancies. Appoint a second person to verify or double check the reconciliation. If you use the services of a bookkeeper, ensure that your oversight procedures adequately cover this person's work.

In addition to ensuring that the bank and the bookkeeper are doing their jobs properly, the self-managing board needs to keep a watchful eye for potential financial problems like a growing list of delinquencies, unpaid bills, cash shortages, budget overruns, and under-funded reserves. This requires constant monitoring of the data listed above in the reports section.

Bonds

Your financial policies should include a requirement that board members and others who handle association funds be appropriately bonded. The association should have a fidelity bond to cover anyone who handles or has access to its funds.

Conflicts of Interest and Kickbacks

When doing business with service providers and professional consultants, always sign a contract or letter of agreement that includes language to the effect that relationships among or between the contractor and members of the self-managing board or other association members that might constitute a conflict of interest must be disclosed.

Similarly the letter of agreement or contract should also state that kickbacks from the contractor aren't allowed and that free services, discounts, or other benefits must benefit the entire association.

Inventories

Association assets include more than cash in the bank. Office equipment, lobby furniture, artwork, tools, and similar items comprise an association's fixed assets. You should inventory these at least once a year. Identify each item with a number, and record its condition, location, and value annually.

◆ ◆ ◆ ◆

Your fiduciary responsibility as a self-managing board is significant. Providing comprehensive information and advice on how to handle your association's finances is beyond the scope of this book, however extensive information is available on this topic. You must educate yourself about the various ways to manage your association's funds in order to protect those funds and yourself.

Related Resources

Collecting Assessments: An Operational Guide, 4th Ed. (GAP Report #10). Community Associations Institute, 1996.

> Collecting money is never easy, but this guide will make a self manager's task as efficient as possible. It provides information on a variety of payment systems and suggests which systems are best for different types and sizes of associations. It also provides numerous practical details on how to implement whatever system you decide on. The section on delinquencies provides a good menu of options to pursue before taking legal action. If it does become necessary to take legal action, GAP 5: *Assessment Collection: Legal Remedies* continues the delinquency discussion where this one ends.

Property Taxes and Homeowner Associations, George R. Grasser (GAP Report #6), Community Associations Institute, 1996.

> While it's best to rely on the expertise of a CPA for all tax matters, self managers will find this report valuable because it provides a general appreciation of the tax issues affecting community associations and puts them in perspective for the layperson. It won't tell you how to do your taxes, but it will give you an understanding, for instance, of why tax assessors—who don't understand community associations—make incorrect property assessments.

The Role of the Association Treasurer (GAP Report #22). Howard A. Goldklang, Community Associations Institute, 1998.

> Although the title suggests this guide is primarily of interest to association treasurers, the financial information it contains will be of interest to all board members. Even if your association uses the services of a CPA, or if your treasurer is a CPA, all board members—especially in self-managed associations—would be advised to have a basic understanding of community association finances.

Chapter 10

Insurance

Obtaining and maintaining proper insurance coverage is a very important aspect of self managing an association. Not only is it an integral part of managing your finances, it also fulfills your duty to preserve the association's property.

Four Exposures to Loss

Your community can suffer from losses in four areas, and insurance is available for most of them. You may have to self-insure, however, for some types of losses. The insurance deductible, for instance, is one form of self-insurance.

1. Property Exposures and Property Insurance

Your association may be responsible for insuring all the residential buildings in your community as well as equipment like lawn mowers or property such as the pool house, and these tangible assets must be protected.

How much and what kind of protection? Legally, how much insurance do you have to purchase? Practically, how much do you *need* to purchase? The answer will depend on whether you live in a planned community, a condominium or a cooperative, so check your governing documents and resolutions, which can be just as binding as recorded documents and may stipulate details such as deductibles.

Next be aware that local, state, and federal statutes may have a bearing on how much and what kinds of insurance your association must have. At the local level, pay attention to building codes and zoning ordinances. For example, if local zoning prohibits rebuilding in your area, the differences between actual cash value and replacement costs become important. The state will require workers compensation and unemployment insurance and the federal government will require Social Security if you employ anyone. And, if your community

---

Other Insurance Coverage Considerations

Consider whether your association needs extra or special coverage in these areas.

- Ordinance and law coverage may provide funds that you need to comply with local requirements.

- Machinery and mechanical equipment coverage might be needed for elevator systems, electrical switch gear, intercom and security systems, pumps and motors, and boilers.

- Earthquake or hurricane coverage might be appropriate depending on your location.

- Pollution and environmental hazard coverage might be needed for cleanup or injury to people.

Insurance Requirements: Five Things to Consider

1. *State Enabling Statute and Corporation Act:* Your condominium, cooperative, or planned community may be subject to a specific state statute. If your association's incorporated, it may also be subject to the requirements of a state non-profit or business corporation statute.

2. *Governing documents:* In general, your governing documents can require more insurance coverage than your enabling statute, but they can't require less. Read your declaration or proprietary lease as well as your rules and regulations for more specific insurance requirements.

3. *Government requirements:* Local, state, and federal statutes sometimes require that you obtain, or at least consider obtaining, certain insurance coverages. At the local level, the most common one is ordinance or law insurance; at the state level, it's workers compensation and employers liability insurance; and, at the federal level, it's the National Flood Insurance Program (NFIP).

4. *Secondary mortgage markets and lender requirements:* FannieMae and FreddieMac, as well as agencies like FHA and VA, may require certain types of insurance before they will buy, insure, or guarantee a mortgage loan in your association. Meeting these requirements may enhance the marketability of units in your community.

5. *Good business judgment:* Even if steps 1–4 don't mention a certain kind of insurance, use your best judgment. The most overlooked insurance coverage is boiler and machinery insurance. It covers mechanical breakdown and electric arcing . Unfortunately, it's usually not mentioned in state statutes or governing documents.

association is located in a flood area, you are required by federal law to participate in the National Flood Insurance Program or your homeowners will not be able to get mortgages from federally insured lenders.

Lenders, agencies, and professional organizations will also require certain levels of insurance coverage before they will do business with your association or people who want to live in it. For example, the Federal National Mortgage Association and the Federal Home Loan Mortgage Corporation will not mortgage homes in associations whose insurance programs don't meet their standards. The same is true of the Federal Housing Administration and Department of Veterans Administration, which will only insure or guarantee mortgages in associations with the required levels of coverage.

What's it worth? Before you can insure the association property, you must determine it's worth. But worth has different meanings, and there are numerous ways to assign it—market value, replacement cost value (RCV), actual cash value (ACV), investment value, and several others. Don't confuse RCV with market value—your homes may be worth much more than it cost to build them, but you can usually only insure for either RCV or ACV.

You, as the insured, are responsible for determining value, and the insurable replacement cost appraisal is the best way to do so. This appraisal becomes very important if your insurance carrier asks the association to sign a statement of value. Once you have paid for the initial cost of such an appraisal it can be updated every year for a nominal fee. (The person doing your reserve study may be able to help you.)

Who's responsible for what? Simplistically speaking, the association generally insures the common areas, and the owners insure their individual units. However, determining where one begins and the other ends is not so simple, and some overlap is inevitable, particularly in condominiums. Based on your governing documents, carefully identify the demarcation, spell it out in the policy by endorsement, and then communicate it to owners—by letter, in your newsletter, at meetings, or by other appropriate means.

What causes property loss? In general, three things cause property to be lost— people, nature, and the economy. People steal or destroy property, neglect or pollute it, or otherwise render it unusable. Nature floods, burns, or blows property away. The economy fluctuates according to factors like technology, strikes, and market conditions. Insurance, however, will protect an association against only the first two types of loss—insofar as possible.

Your property insurance protection is contained in your commercial package policy (which also has your liability and other coverages). The scope of this protection comes in three formats. The most comprehensive coverage for your association is called *Special Form Covered Cause of Loss.* Instead of using the term "peril," property insurance uses the term "covered cause of loss" for things that it insures against like fire and hail.

Exclusions. There are, of course, exclusions to any insurance policy, that is, some occurrences or situations cause losses that are not covered, power failures or military actions, for example. Coverage for some exclusions can be purchased separately. Your basic insurance policy will cover most of what you need—up to a point. After that point, it will either exclude certain things altogether or limit how much loss it will cover for others. There are other types of insurance you can obtain to fill in the gaps or make up the differences in coverage—such as glass insurance, flood insurance, commercial automobile insurance, and even landscaping insurance.

Exclusions

Some losses aren't insurable . . .

- Some events—like war—are so catastrophic that they can't be insured against.
- Some events—like earthquakes or pollution—can't be insured against because insurers can't spread the risks among enough people to cover the costs.
- Some things are simply irreplaceable and this makes them uninsurable.

. . . and others shouldn't be insured at all.

- Some things are better protected by routine maintenance than insurance.
- Some events are covered by another policy.

2. Liability Exposures and Liability Insurance

Your association interprets and enforces governing documents, rules, and resolutions. This leaves the association with a certain amount of liability: residents may take legal action if they believe the association has infringed on their rights in some way. Defending the association can be costly, and losing a suit can be even more costly if damages are awarded. This is an area where liability insurance can add protection.

Probably the most common type of liability for associations comes from what the law calls "negligence." For example, the association may enter a unit unlawfully or fail to remove ice and snow on a walkway. Also, the association can be liable for the acts of others—like a hired security guard.

A commercial general liability (CGL) policy will cover many of these exposures. However, it won't cover the association if the injury or damage was intentional or if it was caused by a wrong act or omission—which is why you need directors and officers liability insurance. Neither will it cover incidents that could be covered by some other type of insurance—like workers compensation and employers liability insurance or auto insurance. There are other exclusions like injuries resulting from the work of professionals or from damage caused by pollutants. Review your policy carefully with your insurance representative to ensure you are familiar with what's included and what isn't.

Some states, copying the federal government, have limitations on tort liability for volunteers who serve on nonprofit boards. This type of protection, unfortunately, usually doesn't apply to serving on the board of a community association. Even if there's a limitation on damages, your defense costs can still be significant. Liability insurance pays for most legal defense costs.

3. Net Income Exposures and Income Insurance

Some insurers offer coverage for loss of assessment income from a covered cause of loss. Check with your agent. Some communities rent out a garage space or have laundry machine income. This type of income can be insured.

Business income insurance usually also has "extra expense" protection as well. For instance, boiler and machinery insurance, with the addition of business income and extra expense protection, will pay for the cost of a portable generator in the event the boiler breaks down.

4. Personnel Exposures and Personnel Insurance

Most associations face two types of losses. The first is from theft of money and the second is from injury to individuals hired to do work.

Your association can insure against theft of association funds with fidelity insurance, and it's important that your fidelity insurance policy includes an endorsement for non-compensated volunteers so that the association is covered if a board or committee member is the thief.

Most small self-managed associations have no employees so they assume they don't need workers compensation and employers liability insurance. However, if the association employs a contractor who fails to carry this coverage and one of the contractor's employees is injured, the association might be considered a co-employer or employer of the injured worker. Your community can obtain this coverage on an "if any employee" basis.

Your agent can help you with the risk management necessary to identify your exposures to loss in these four areas. Once they have been identified, then you, your agent, and the insurance company can develop a comprehensive insurance program for your community.

One coverage, however, deserves more extended discussion—directors and officers liability insurance (D&O). Your governing documents probably require your association to indemnify and hold harmless your board members for most types of legal liability. D&O can help fund that requirement.

Directors & Officers Liability Insurance

All boards are exposed to personal and corporate liability, and self-managing boards should pay particular attention to protecting themselves. Claims have been brought against board members for discrimination, enforcing rules selectively, wrongful termination, mismanaging funds, even for denying architectural plans. Obviously, some type of protection is needed, and it comes in the form of Directors and Officers (D&O) insurance. A good D&O policy should cover all current and past directors and officers and anyone else acting on the board's behalf, such as committee members. It won't cover acts of outright dishonestly or personal profit, and it may also exclude sexual harassment, discrimination, and wrongful discharge.

You can get D&O insurance rolled in with your property and liability coverage in one package policy. It's tempting because it's less expensive than buying individual D&O coverage, but package policies may have lots of exclusions. Also, package policies may restrict the definition of "insured" to directors and officers only, leaving out committee members and volunteers acting for the board.

Why D&O?

You'll need D&O if you've got to defend yourself against any number of allegations.

- Failing to carry out obligations specified in the governing documents.
- Treating association members unequally.
- Violating fair-housing requirements.
- Imposing assessments wrongfully.
- Harassing members.
- Conducting business secretly.
- Discriminating against residents or potential residents.

Finding the Best Insurance Company

Don't decide on insurance by price alone. The insurance company and the insurance agent you work with should be able to convince you of three things:

1. They provide the best and most comprehensive coverages, in compliance with your legal obligations and your exposures to loss, that are available in the insurance marketplace.

2. They have experienced staff and field personnel to help you administer your insurance program including coming to the annual meeting to explain that program and to help unit owners determine what type of insurance they need for their homes.

3. They are price competitive with other insurers who provide insurance programs for community associations.

Begin by purchasing a policy from a company that has lots of experience with community associations. This ensures that the people you work with understand the peculiar needs of your association and have experience processing claims similar to yours.

You can get insurance from private providers or from the government. In most cases, you have a choice whether to obtain insurance, but in some instances you will be required to obtain it. Often, the insurance that is required by law must be obtained from the government—but not always.

You will want to get your insurance from a licensed insurer that holds a high rating from A.M. Best, Standard & Poor, or similar organizations. You can get insurance from an unlicensed insurer, but you won't have the protection of state backed funds if it goes under. On the other hand, if you can't get a particular type of coverage from a licensed insurer, the unlicensed insurer may be an acceptable alternative.

What Should Be In Your D&O Policy?

- Covers past and present directors, officers, committee members, volunteers, trustees, and employees
- Covers the association named in the definition of insured
- Does not exclude prior acts
- Covers the builder/developer while serving on the board
- Defends non-monetary damages
- Does not exclude sexual harassment, discrimination, and wrongful discharge
- Does not exclude libel, slander, and defamation of character
- Does not exclude publishers' liability and copyright infringement
- Provides a duty to defend
- Carries an A.M. Best rating of at least an "A"

(From "Things You Need to Know When Buying D&O," Common Ground, *July/August 1996)*

By conducting routine maintenance operations, boards meet their duty to protect the property from normal use and aging. However, only by obtaining appropriate and adequate insurance coverage, do you meet your duty to protect the association from natural catastrophe, crime, and lawsuits.

Related Resources

Community Association Insurance: A Guide for Condominium, Cooperatives, and Planned Communities, 4th Ed. (GAP Report #4), Treese & Rosenberry. Community Associations Institute, 1997.

> Self managers seeking in-depth information about community association insurance will find this resource particularly helpful. It answers important questions you might not think to ask. The section on property insurance is particularly useful because it examines the ever-vexing question of common element and limited common element overlap. It also provides information on owner's insurance—not necessarily an association responsibility, but very informative for a self manager.

Community Association Risk Management: Evaluating and Managing Risk in Condominiums, Co-ops, and Planned Communities, 2nd Ed. (GAP Report #25), Clifford J. Treese, CPCU, ARM. Community Associations Institute, 1998.

> A companion and natural follow on to GAP Report #4, this report explains the integral relationship between insurance and risk management. Chapters on establishing a risk management program and administering claims are particularly helpful because they provide detail beyond the scope of *Self-Management.*

Chapter 11

The Public Policy Process

Community associations today face more legislative, regulatory, and legal challenges than ever before. The number of laws, regulations, codes, court decisions, and administrative actions impacting community associations is at an all-time high. For self-managing boards especially, the need to be aware of and involved in the public policy process must seem daunting. When you're required to be a financial expert, contracts manager, event planner, social worker, rules enforcer, and overall administrator—*after* you come home from your day job—public policy involvement may be near the bottom of your list. This is especially true if you'd also like to have some sort of personal life.

However, ignoring the importance of public policy is a risky proposition when simple changes to tax or bankruptcy laws might cause your association to lose—or gain—hundreds of thousands of dollars.

The overall increase in the number of community associations presents an enlarged target for legislative initiatives; and, indeed, bills impacting community associations are on the rise. Many are discussed in this book and include the Fair Housing Act Amendments, the Housing for Older Persons Act, the Americans with Disabilities Act, the Bankruptcy Reform Act, and the Telecommunications Act, among others.

Like the federal government, state and local governments are also focusing more on community associations. There are numerous reasons for this increased attention.

Community association housing is growing and maturing. As a result, problems in existing laws are being identified and addressed—whether effectively or not. Also, new issues—real or imagined—are being tackled, sometimes appropriately and other times with little need or forethought.

Federalism is popular again. Shifting power and programs back to the states became a popular tool a few years ago for federal lawmakers facing staggering deficits and strained budgets. This shift has empowered state and local lawmakers who, like their federal counterparts, are increasingly behind legislative and regulatory proposals that raise concerns for you and other community association leaders.

State and local governments are more professional—and active. As populations have grown, many state and local legislative, executive, and judicial bodies have increased in size and sophistication. In many cases, this means the number of laws and regulations has increased as well enabling legislators to micromanage your basic association functions.

Networking among legislators has resulted in more legislation. Communication among lawmakers has increased. State and local officials participate in several national groups where they regularly share philosophies and model legislation. Proposals in one state appear almost simultaneously in others.

Technology has enabled others to organize and engage in the legislative process. Just as e-mail and Web sites better allow you and your fellow community association homeowners to communicate with government officials, so too can any party seeking action that might be contrary to your interests.

The expansion of state and local authority is apparent today, even on issues that are also being debated at the federal level. Despite several years of debate in Congress, electric utility deregulation—an issue that will financially impact every community association and every homeowner—is moving primarily as a result of state actions across the country. Also, more states are becoming the battlegrounds for telecommunications forced-entry legislation since providers have thus far been unsuccessful in getting federal officials to trample community associations' private property rights. While most of these assaults on you and your neighbors have been turned back, telecommunications providers continue to wage an intensive campaign betting that their influence with state legislators will outweigh your ability to respond.

Simple Steps for Getting Involved

How federal, state, and local matters ultimately impact your association will depend on whether you are or are *not* involved in the process to shape them. While such involvement may sound daunting, there are a number of fairly simple yet important steps that volunteer managers can take to stay abreast of, prepare for, and influence governmental decisions impacting your association. For example:

Commit your association's demographics to paper. Take the time to gather the following statistics; list them neatly on your association letterhead, or create an attractive one-page handout.

- Name, size, and age of your community
- Number of homes or units
- Number of residents
- Amount of assessments collected
- Amount of taxes paid
- Annual budget
- Value of property (common and individual)
- Voting percentage of residents (if available)
- Local, state, and federal political districts
- Community and charitable activities of the association

This information, and other data that demonstrates the significance of your community and its residents, should be summarized and available before you need to use it. The need will arise. Take time now to prepare.

Educate board members, staff, and residents. Teach them the importance of participating in the public policy process and the real world implications of laws, regulations, codes, court decisions, and administration actions on their quality of life and finances. In a legislative battle, you will need a solid grassroots structure. Organize it now!

Form a government affairs committee in your association. A committee can be a visible and dependable source of information as well as an important first line of defense when needed. Members can divide responsibilities to track important issues at all levels of government, establish ties to other organizations in the community that have similar concerns or have resources your association could share. Committee members can educate residents and get them involved or prepared to act if needed. The job of this committee will be much easier and members will be far more effective if they participate in the government and public affairs programs provided by CAI. (See Community Associations Advocacy Network below.)

Establish relationships with relevant local, state, and federal government officials. Invite officials to your community to meet the residents (the voters). Such visits provide a wonderful opportunity to educate legislators and regulators about what community associations are and how legislation and regulations impact your association. A visit or tour also starts building relationships that will be needed in the future.

Take advantage of government mailing lists. Identify the government bodies that can impact your community, and ask to be added to their mailing lists for meeting notices, or for copies of proposed ordinances, laws, or regulations. Even if you can't attend every meeting, you'll know what issues are being considered and when to mobilize your neighbors.

Use technology. Almost every government office today has a Web site and e-mail capability. Find the Web or e-mail address of your local, state, and federal representatives and agencies of interest. To identify federal lawmakers, you can utilize the CAI Advocacy Center in the government affairs section of CAI's Web site at www.caionline.org or visit Thomas, the Web site for the U.S. Congress, at www.thomas.loc.gov/. Additional links for tracking your government at work are included at the end of this chapter.

Cultivate relationships with reporters for print and electronic media. Just as with government officials, you need media reporters who understand your association. Solid relationships with the media will help your voice be heard when important issues break and improve your ability to respond should a crisis erupt.

Participate in the Community Associations Institute (CAI) through membership and events. Take advantage of the best resource available to keep you informed about federal, state, and local issues of concern to community associations. CAI not only tracks developments, but also provides a vehicle for you to become involved in the political process. Local chapter meetings, state

Online Resources for State & Federal Offices & Agencies

Community Associations Information

Community Associations Institute
www.caionline.org

Congressional Information

Thomas (Library of Congress Legis. Information)
www.thomas.loc.gov

Legislative Branch Resource Site
www.lcweb.loc.gov/global/
legislative/congress.html

United States House of Representatives
www.house.gov

United States Senate
www.senate.gov

Federal Courts

Federal Courts Site
www.uscourts.gov

United States Courts of Appeal
(Cornell University)
www.secure.law.cornell.edu/
federal/opinions.html

United States Supreme Court
(Cornell University)
supct.law.cornell.edu/supct

Federal Govt. Departments & Agencies

Department of Housing & Urban Development
www.hud.gov

Federal Communications Commission
www.fcc.gov

Federal Govt. Information & Publications

Code of Federal Regulations
www.access.gpo.gov/nara/cfr/
index.html

Congressional Record
www.access.gpo.gov/su_docs/
aces/aces150.html

Consumer Gateway
www.consumer.gov

Federal Register
www.access.gpo.gov/su_docs/
aces/aces140.html

Federal Statutes
(Cornell University)
www.law.cornell.edu/statutes.
html

FedNet
www.fednet.net

Fedstats
www.fedstats.gov

Fedworld Information Network
www.fedworld.gov

Government Information Locator Service
www.access.gpo.gov/su_docs/
gils/gils.html

Govt. Resources on the Web
(U of Michigan)
www.lib.umich.edu/libhome/
Documents.center/govweb.html

Library of Congress
www.loc.gov/

U. S. Federal Govt. Agencies Directory (Louisiana State U.)
www.lib.lsu.edu/gov/fedgov.html

Locating Federal Legislators

CAI Advocacy Center
congress.nw.dc.us/cai

CapWeb
www.capweb.net/classic/index.
morph

Contacting the Congress
www.visi.com/juan/congress/
cgi-bin

State & Local Govt. Information & Publications

State and Local Gateway
www.statelocal.gov/

State & Local Government Resource Sites
lcweb.loc.gov/global/state/
stategov.html

State & Local Government Site Locator
www.piperinfo.com/state/states.
html

State Statutes (Cornell University)
www.law.cornell.edu/statutes.html

Legislative Action Committees, and national conferences and seminars help you learn how specific challenges and opportunities may affect your association. The resources available through membership—from advocacy and education to publications and networking—exist nowhere else and offer you a substantial return on a modest investment of dues dollars.

Join the Community Associations Advocacy Network (CAAN). One of the best ways to get involved is to join the CAAN grassroots program. CAAN members are kept apprised of issues important to community associations and are informed about how to communicate with legislators to advocate the community association position. CAAN membership is free to all CAI members and anyone whose association, firm, or company is a member of CAI. You can join by visiting the CAAN area of the government affairs section of CAI's Web site at www.caionline.org or by contact CAI's Government & Public Affairs Department at 703-548-8600.

Federal, state, and local government officials are positioned as never before as decision makers on issues affecting community associations. Your political involvement with these public officials can help make a difference for community associations. The straightforward steps outlined above can help you engage in the public policy process, remain aware of the most important issues facing community associations, and prepare residents to act when they're most needed.

Part III: Legal Considerations

Chapter 12

Fair Housing

The federal Fair Housing Amendments Act of 1988 (FHAA) provides protections for families with children and for the disabled. Self managers need to understand these protections and enforce them.

Families With Children

Community associations can't discriminate against families with children under 18 years of age unless they qualify as housing for older persons.

Housing for Older Persons

The only exception to the "familial status discrimination" consideration is what is properly called "housing for older persons."

You can't simply decide that your community association will be for older persons and won't allow children. According to federal law, you must meet three conditions in order to qualify as housing for older persons.

1. At least 80 percent of the occupied units must have at least one person 55 years of age or older.

2. The community association must publish and adhere to rules and regulations that support the community's intent to provide housing for older persons.

3. The community association must verify the age of its occupants, no less frequently than every two years, and in accordance with Department of Housing and Urban Development (HUD) regulations.

So long as your community association can demonstrate that it satisfies these three requirements, it can turn away families with children without violating federal law.

Appropriate Rules and Regulations

Demonstrating that 80 percent of the units in your community are occupied by at least one person over 55 years of age is relatively simple. But determining what rules and regulations support the commu-

Forms of Familial Status Discrimination

- Turning away prospective residents because of their children
- Fining or singling out families because of the activities of their children
- Enacting rules that unfairly segregate or restrict use of common areas by children
- Statements by board members against children
- Limits on the number of persons who may occupy a unit
- Requiring residents to be related by blood or marriage

nity's intent to provide housing for older persons is a little more challenging. HUD believes that your governing documents indicate whether your community has the appropriate intent to provide senior housing. How you advertise or hold yourself out to the public also indicates your intent, as well as how consistently you apply the age restrictions.

Ensure that your association's restrictions follow federal law. They should require that at least 80 percent of the units have one resident 55 years of age or older. You can avoid coming near the 80 percent level by requiring that 100 percent of the units have at least one resident 55 or older. Federal law doesn't specify ages for other residents, so you could specify that all residents must be 55 or older or you could specify nothing for the other residents.

You may find it difficult to amend your governing documents to follow federal law on this point because you need a high number of votes or consent from lenders. If you try to remove incorrect language from your governing documents, HUD will consider your "good faith attempt." Be sure to carefully document your efforts and maintain evidence of your activities.

> ## Use Rules That Do NOT Discriminate
>
> **Do**
> - Enact rules that focus on behavior.
> - Enact rules that are reasonably related to health and safety.
>   *Example:* Swimmers must demonstrate proficiency or swim with a companion.
>
> **Don't**
> - Enact rules that focus on age.
> - Enact rules that are a disguise for discrimination.
>   *Example:* Children under 8 are not allowed in the pool.

Strike any reference in your governing documents, signs, or advertisements that refer to your community as an "adult" or "active adult" community. HUD believes these terms indicate that you intend to discriminate, rather than to provide senior housing. Appropriate terms would include "55+," "55 or better," "senior housing," or "housing for older persons."

The Other 20 Percent

Sometimes a developer, or residents, will argue that 20 percent of your association's units can be held for families with children or other non-seniors. This isn't true. The 20 percent is a margin that allows you some flexibility in enforcement. Additionally, reserving 20 percent of your units for families with children would be inconsistent with the association's desire to provide housing for older persons.

Verifying Age

You'll need to maintain evidence that verifies the ages of your residents. Photocopies of drivers' licenses, birth certificates, or similar documents are acceptable evidence. This information is extremely private, so you have a responsibility to keep it away from the public and members of the association. When asked, you need only supply a summary of the information. The only exception is that you would be required to produce this evidence if your association was involved in fair housing legal proceedings.

Your Liability

Self managers face a substantial liability when attempting to enforce a community's restrictions. You may be accused of discriminating against families with children. The FHAA provides you with some protection in the form of the good faith defense. If you believe the association qualifies for the housing for older persons exemption and you know that the association has asserted in writing that it qualifies, then you aren't liable in money damages to the victims of unlawful familial-status discrimination. In order to take advantage of the defense, your association's governing body should assert in writing annually that it qualifies for the housing for older persons exemption. And, to make sure you and the other volunteer managers have actual knowledge of the assertion, you should sign and date it.

Discrimination Against the Disabled

The FHAA prohibits you from discriminating on the basis of disability. Disability (or handicap, the word actually used in the FHAA) is very broadly defined, and it includes both physical and mental disabilities. You cannot discriminate against a person who has a disability, or associates with a disabled person, or who appears to be disabled.

Making Reasonable Accommodations

The FHAA requires you to make "reasonable accommodations" in the rules, policies, practices, or services of the association where necessary to permit a disabled person to use and enjoy their unit and the common areas. The FHAA does not provide a list of reasonable accommodations. You are expected to explore the possibilities with the resident. Once a resident (or associate of the resident) mentions that he or she is disabled, and that some change in the rules or facilities may be needed, the burden shifts to the association to explore what might be a reasonable accommodation. Making reasonable accommodations may sometimes seem to conflict with your obligation to enforce association rules evenhandedly, so complying with these laws will be challenging.

You don't have to do everything possible for accommodations to be reasonable. The resident's needs should be weighed against the burden on your association to make modifications. Whether a major structural alteration might be unreasonable, for example, depends to some extent on the cost to the association. The issue gets a little less clear as the difference between reasonable accommodation and reasonable modification fades.

What's reasonable will differ from case to case. For example, the exorbitant cost of replacing an unreliable elevator may not be reasonable, but the cost of a service contract certainly is.

Parking, Pets, and Making Modifications

For community associations, reasonable accommodations most commonly involve parking, pets, and modifications of the unit or common areas.

Parking. You must provide reserved parking spaces to disabled residents upon request even when space is scarce—unless you can prove that creating a handicapped parking space would be an unreasonable thing to do to the other residents, which is unlikely.

If parking is assigned, you may not be able to accommodate a request to reserve a handicapped space. The space simply doesn't belong to the association. But, assuming that the resident requesting the accommodation has a regular space assigned, it's likely the issue is its location and proximity to the resident's home. In this instance, you may need to reassign parking to permit a disabled person to have a parking space close to his or her unit.

When all parking spaces are owned in common by all members of the association, the association probably has the authority to reserve handicapped parking spaces.

Pets. The FHAA requires that you permit disabled residents to have service animals to assist them in using and enjoying their dwelling. Normally, the first step is determining whether the resident requesting an exception to the no-pet policy has a disability. According to the FHAA, a person with a disability has a physical or mental impairment that substantially limits one or more major life activities like walking, seeing, and breathing. It can also apply to a person merely regarded as having a disability. The disability doesn't have to be obvious or even observable. The scope of the definition is fairly broad, although the condition must be one that substantially limits a major life activity. Normally a temporary condition or one that is relatively minor, like normal allergies, won't be considered a disability. Recent court decisions have also limited who is disabled. Courts will look at a condition in its *treated* state. Therefore, someone who is legally blind isn't disabled if glasses correct the blindness. Stated another way, the person is only disabled if he or she is legally blind even *with* glasses. Similarly, if someone who is mentally disabled can function normally when under medication, the person would probably not be considered disabled.

To qualify as a service animal, the animal should serve a function related to the resident's disability. For instance, a sight-impaired person wouldn't be entitled to an animal that's strictly a pet—the animal must actually assist the blind. If the animal isn't a nuisance, courts are likely to find association prohibitions against them unreasonable. On the other hand, if an animal is uncontrollable, it isn't reasonable to accommodate it.

If your association has a no-pets or restricted-pets policy, consider adding language that supports the rights of residents with disabilities to have a service animal and to entertain guests with disabilities accompanied by service animals. This helps eliminate misunderstanding and confusion for other residents.

Modifying Units or Common Areas. When the unit or common area needs to be modified, your association may require that the modification be safe, properly permitted, and comply with your architectural guidelines. Be sure that the architectural approval process does not cause undue delays or become an excuse to deny an otherwise reasonable request. If you need more information (such as blueprints or information on a disability) let the applicant know as quickly as possible, and try to arrange for a temporary accommodation until the situation is resolved. Do not ask for a security deposit or require any payment in order to approve an architectural modification.

Sample Language

Pet Policies Regarding Service Animals

The Willow Oaks Community Association subscribes to the principles set forth in the federal Fair Housing Act protecting the rights of people with disabilities to use and enjoy their homes. The association will make reasonable accommodations for residents who request service animals.

OR

Service animals are exempt from the Willow Oaks Community Association pet policy.

In addition to accommodating pets, parking, and modifications, remember also that you need to keep up the common areas in a manner that allows people access to their homes. For example, if the association fails to shovel snow from sidewalks, residents in wheelchairs or those who walk with the aid of canes or braces may not be able to get to their homes.

What to Ask For

If you're approached before a disabled person becomes a resident, don't ask questions regarding the disability unless and until the prospective resident (or his or her associates) brings it up. Only after the possibility of an accommodation has been mentioned should you discuss the nature of the request.

After a disabled person has become a resident and requested an accommodation, you can request confirmation of the disability and of the need for the accommodation. Many associations accept a signed physician's certificate containing the necessary information, and they ask for periodic re-certifications.

Protections for Self Managers

When it comes to the FHAA, your challenge is to prevent people who aren't disabled from taking advantage of the association while also providing every means for those who are to enjoy their homes. While you'll likely err on the side of caution, it's still possible the association may be accused of discrimination.

People who believe they are victims of unlawful housing discrimination have numerous avenues of recourse. They can file a claim with HUD, the state equivalent of HUD, a federal court, or a state court. According to the FHAA, if they win a case against your association, not only would you have to reverse the discrimination, but the association would also have to pay their attorney's fees and compensate them monetarily for damages such as higher rent or house payments in another community. You might also have to pay punitive damages if your association has repeatedly violated the FHAA over a long period of time.

Don't count on your insurance to cushion a blow like this. Your coverage for violations of the FHAA is extremely limited. Nevertheless, you should review your insurance policy carefully to ensure that you have the fullest available coverage to protect you against accusations of discrimination. Directors and officers liability insurance policies will exclude you from coverage for intentional wrongful acts and violations of civil rights. Therefore, you must familiarize yourself with fair housing issues and develop sources of information for your difficult questions. You can do this by contacting your local fair housing council, which may offer presentations or provide other sources of education and information.

Remember, when you speak as a board member, you speak for the entire association. So, if you discriminate unlawfully—even unintentionally—you may create a liability for the entire community. For example, a casual comment by a director to a prospective resident that the community had very few children was deemed by the courts to indicate intent to discriminate against families with children. Therefore, you should consider removing board members or other volunteers who display little control or make inflammatory or prejudiced remarks. This will limit your association's exposure in litigation.

Maintain complete records that show that disabled residents and families with children are treated in the same fashion as other residents or applicants for residency. Like other private records, maintain these in confidence, and disclose them only as required by law.

Consult your association's attorney on these difficult issues. This is an area where the law is new and developing at a fairly rapid pace. Choose an attorney with expertise in the area, given the potential for money damages not covered by insurance.

◆ ◆ ◆ ◆

Some or all of the protections of the FHAA may seem unfair to associations. Remember that Congress concluded, after lengthy hearings, that these protections were required in order to permit vulnerable members of society to enjoy the same rights and privileges as others. If your association is adequately aware of the law and committed to complying with it, your community will be stronger and better integrated in the future.

Related Resources

Aging in Place: The Development of Naturally Occurring Retirement Communities. Ellen Hirsch de Haan, Community Associations Institute, 1996.

> The question of changing demographics shouldn't be overlooked by self managing boards—whether within the context of the fair housing act or otherwise. The implications for associations of aging populations are significant, and this book provides a valuable overview of the nature and scope of the situation. Self managers will find it's practical and positive approach to accommodating aging residents refreshing and inspiring.

Pet Policies: How To Draft and Enforce Rules That Sit, Stay, and Heel. Debra H. Lewin. (GAP Report #28), Community Associations Institute, 2001.

> Besides the considerations raised by the fair housing act about service animals, the larger issue of regulating pets in community associations seems to be an ongoing question. GAP 28 discusses this question at some length and offers solutions and ideas that self managers may find helpful.

Chapter 13

Antenna Rules

There are numerous federal regulations that affect community associations; but, perhaps the ones that come close to home most often are antenna rules. Congress believes that the public should have widespread access to video programming, so these rules state that community associations can't prohibit or restrict residents from installing television aerials or satellite dishes.

The Telecommunications Act

The Telecommunications Act of 1996 supercedes your governing documents if they restrict your residents' ability to receive television signals—that is, if they restrict satellite dishes and antennae. The Telecommunications Act gave the Federal Communications Commission (FCC) the authority to regulate how all this will work.

Basically, the FCC says that if a resident directly or indirectly owns or leases a unit that he or she alone uses or controls, your association may not:

- unreasonably delay or prevent the use of certain types of antennas
- unreasonably increase the cost of certain types of antennas
- prevent the resident from receiving an acceptable quality signal from certain types of antennas

Only if your restriction addresses a legitimate safety concern or the restriction is necessary for historic preservation would there be an exception to these rules.

Central Antennas

One of the things you can do to prevent residents from installing their own antennas is to provide owners in one building with a common antenna. If your association chooses to do this, make sure that:

- The residents get the service they want and would have gotten with their own individual antennas.
- The signal quality is as good as, or

What Does the FCC Consider an Antenna?

- Satellite dishes one meter (approximately 40") or less in diameter
- Antennas that receive video programming by multi-point distribution services (wireless cable) that are one meter or less in diameter
- Television aerial antennas that receive signals over the air
- Masts are currently causing some confusion, but the FCC considers them a type of antenna.

better than, the residents would have gotten with their own individual antennas.

- The residents don't have to pay more for the central antenna than they would have paid for the installation, maintenance, and use of their own individual antennas.

- The requirement to use the central antenna doesn't unreasonably delay the viewer's ability to receive the video programming desired. In other words, you must be able to install the central antenna and deliver programming to the residents about as quickly as other service providers could have installed an individual antenna.

- If your central antenna doesn't provide programming that a resident wants, you must modify the central antenna or install another one in a reasonable time, or allow the residents to install their own antennas.

Some associations have rules that are more restrictive than others because property rights differ among detached home communities, town home developments, and condominiums.

Condominium owners have an interest in the common property along with the other owners; however, they don't have exclusive use or control of the roof or exterior wall of the building. Therefore, they cannot install an antenna on the roof if your association says no. Residents can, however, install antennas on private patios, balconies, or yards because they have exclusive use these common areas.

Town house residents have exclusive use of their chimneys, even if the association maintains, repairs, or replaces the outside of the building or the roof. Therefore, according to the FCC, they can install antennas on the chimney. Your association can require the resident to remove the dish temporarily to maintain or repair the roof, and you can take steps to protect your association by asking for indemnification. However, you can't prohibit the installation.

Many community associations have restricted-access areas such as the roof. Residents generally don't have exclusive control or use of these areas if the association is responsible for maintenance and repair. Therefore, your association can restrict residents from drilling holes or otherwise piercing restricted-access areas without the association's consent.

Property Damage

If one of your residents damages a common area or injures someone while installing, maintaining, or using an antenna, he or she is liable for that damage. Furthermore, your association can require the resident to indemnify the association against liability arising from installing, maintaining, or using a dish located within his or her exclusive area.

Unreasonable Delays and Expenses

Your community association may have certain procedures for approving antenna installations. The FCC says that, in general, permit and approval requirements cause unreasonable delay and expense. For example, if you ask a resident to submit an application form, a permit fee, a plot plan showing the location and size of the antenna, and a certificate from a dealer or installer identifying signal reception locations, that's unreasonable. The only exceptions are valid safety concerns or historic preservation. You should carefully examine your association's architectural review and approval procedures for antennas and make sure you comply with the FCC rules.

Unreasonable Installation Costs

There are no formulas or percentages specifying what costs are reasonable or unreasonable for installing, maintaining, and using antennas. Nevertheless, the FCC requires that whatever it costs a resident to comply with your association's restrictions not be "unreasonable in light of the cost of the equipment or services and the rule, law, regulation, or restriction's treatment of comparable devices." This doesn't provide much guidance; but, bear in mind that the FCC considers a $5 permit fee an "unwarranted charge."

Some examples may be helpful. The FCC states that your association can't require a resident to screen relatively "unobtrusive" DBS antennas by "expensive" landscaping; however, you can require a resident to paint an antenna as long as it doesn't interfere with reception or increase costs.

The FCC says that your association can't require an owner to use a professional contractor to install an antenna (unless safety or historic preservations make it necessary). However, if a resident does use a contractor, your association can require the contractor to have insurance for personal injuries or structural damage. You can't require the resident to get an additional insured endorsement from the contractor. Also, your association can't require a resident to hire a contractor to certify that an installation meets your guidelines.

> **What Are Valid Safety Restrictions?**
> **Acceptable Restrictions:**
> - Minimum distances from power lines
> - Specified distances from trees and intersections that provide a clear line of sight for drivers
> - Adequate bolting or guying
> - Mast heights and setbacks
>
> **Unacceptable Restrictions:**
> - Barring antennas over a certain height

Acceptable Signal Quality

Your association can regulate where residents place their antennas as long as the rules don't impair reception or increase the residents' cost. The FCC says that, if the rule causes signal reception to be "impossible or . . . substantially degraded," then it's invalid.

For example, your association can require residents to place their antennas where they can't be seen from the street, as long as that doesn't impair signal reception or increase costs. In a dispute, your association must prove that the resident can get good reception at your specified location, rather than the resident proving that he or she cannot.

Your association must clearly define the health or safety objective in your restriction or a document easily available to your residents. Furthermore, restrictions can't be any more burdensome than necessary to achieve those objectives.

Antenna Policies

If your association establishes policies or restrictions on antennas, be sure to address your community's particular needs. This is necessary because ownership interests differ, and home sites and community topography can affect signal quality. Be sure to have your association counsel review whatever policies you decide on to make sure they are consistent with FCC rules. The FCC's rulings in this area are evolving, and so they change from time to time. So, you should also have your attorney review old policies periodically.

If your policy permits the association to set reasonable screening or location requirements on a case-by-case basis, the policy should specifically state that the term "reasonable" means requirements that will not impose unreasonable expense or delay or preclude reception of an acceptable quality signal.

Violations

If your association or a resident goes to court or files a petition over an antenna restriction, the FCC has certain procedures and limitations on enforcement. For example, fines can't accrue and attorney's fees can't be assessed while the validity of your restriction is pending before the FCC or the court, but an initial fine can be imposed if the restriction is ultimately upheld.

Considering the complexity of the FCC rules and residents' demands for programming, it's important for self managers to be well aware of the nature and intent of the FCC's antenna rules. It's also important to rely on an attorney experienced in community association law if you have specific questions or when a resident and the association don't agree.

Related Resource

The Community Association's Guide to Telecommunications Management: Getting Connected. Howley & Clark, Community Associations Institute, 1999.

> Those who want more detail about the FCC's antenna rules will find that this book is quite comprehensive, but also easy to understand. Self managers who don't yet have antenna policies in place might want to take advantage of the model documents; those who do may want to compare documents. Also, if local cable providers approach your association with licensing agreements this book can help you protect the association's interests.

Chapter 14

Fair Debt Collection

T he federal Fair Debt Collection Practices Act (FDCPA) has made abusive debt collection practices illegal. However, it only applies to those who regularly collect debts owed to another. Thus, the FDCPA doesn't apply to self-managed associations. However, your self-managed association may be subject to state debt collection statutes. Since most state provisions are similar to the federal act, you will need a thorough understanding of the FDCPA. You or your association attorney should review your state's FDCPA to ensure that your association is complying. To be safe, you should comply with the FDCPA whether or not it applies to your association.

You can't communicate anything that is false, deceptive, or misleading. For example, you should never tell a debtor that legal action has been taken or imply that you are an attorney when that isn't true. Nor should you threaten legal action unless you definitely intend to take it. The courts will look at your statements through the eyes of the "least sophisticated debtor."

There are steps you can take to show that you intend to follow through with an action against a debtor. Send a warning letter explaining your intended collection action. Be sure to say you "intend to" take action, not that you "will" take action. Although you fully intend to take action at the time you send the warning letter, circumstances change, and you may

States That Have Fair Debt Collection Laws

California	Maine	Pennsylvania
Colorado	Maryland	South Carolina
Connecticut	Massachusetts	Texas
District of Columbia	Michigan	Vermont
Florida	New Hampshire	West Virginia
Hawaii	New York	Wisconsin
Iowa	North Carolina	
Louisiana	Oregon	

change your position. This subtle difference in language may protect you when this happens.

Your association may be contacted by third parties who are trying to help a delinquent owner pay his or her debt. Unless the debtor or a court has given you permission, you may not communicate with that third party regarding the debt. You should probably ask the delinquent owner for that consent in writing before dealing with a third party. Also, if you are contacting an owner and need to leave a message, either with another person or on an answering machine, don't mention that the call involves collecting a debt.

If you are communicating with someone in order to locate the debtor, make sure you do the following:

- Identify yourself and state that you're confirming or correcting location information about the resident.
- Tell the person who you're working for if you're asked.
- Don't state that the person owes a debt.
- Don't contact anyone more than once asking about the location of the debtor unless they ask you or unless you believe the information you got previously was wrong or incomplete, and the person now has correct information.
- Don't indicate on your correspondence or on the envelope that your correspondence deals with collecting a debt.
- Don't correspond by postcard.
- Don't try to locate the debtors once you know they're represented by an attorney, if you can readily ascertain the attorney's name and address.
- Don't ask for post-dated checks if your state prohibits it.
- Indicate in your correspondence that your association is a debt collector if your state requires it.

Avoid Harassment and Abuse When Collecting Debts

- Don't use or threaten violence or criminal harm
- Don't use obscene or abusive language
- Don't publish the names of residents who refuse to pay
- Don't advertise a debt for sale to coerce payment
- Don't call a person repeatedly to annoy them
- Don't fail to let the debtor know who you are

Failure to Comply

If you fail to comply with the federal act, you will be liable for statutory fines as well as damages for emotional distress or slander and additional damages. You may also have to pay the defendant's attorney's fees and the costs of the action, if the court finds that you brought the action in bad faith to harass the debtor.

To decide whether you violated the act, a court will look at how often and how persistently you broke the rules and how many debtors you harassed. You won't be held liable if you can prove that you didn't intend to violate the act and that you made an honest mistake despite having procedures in place to prevent the error.

◆ ◆ ◆ ◆

The FDCPA requirements that you have to observe may compromise your ability to pursue debtors who are delinquent with their assessments, even though a question remains in some courts whether assessments are actually debts. Efforts are underway to reform the act to exclude community association assessments from the definition of debt, but until the law is settled on this issue, you should comply with debt collection laws in order to avoid liability.

How to Communicate with Debtors (According to the FDCPA)

What is "Communication" With a Debtor?
- Written (letters or correspondence)
- Verbal—phone conversations
- Messages—voice mail, answering machines, left with someone else

When and Where Should You Communicate?
- Contact the debtor between 8:00 a.m. and 9:00 p.m. Communication before or after these hours is considered inconvenient to the debtor and isn't allowed.
- Don't communicate with the debtor at an unusual place. For example, don't communicate with a debtor at work if you know the employer prohibits such calls, or if the debtor has asked you not to call at work.

Who Should You Contact?
- If you know an attorney represents a debtor and you can reasonably locate the attorney, you must contact the attorney, not the debtor.

Are There Any Exceptions?
- Yes, if the debtor has given you prior written consent or a court has given you permission.

When Should You Stop Communicating?
- When the debtor notifies you in writing that he or she will not pay the debt or wants no further communication with you, then you must stop your communication. However, you can advise the debtor that you are pursuing ordinary collection actions, taking legal action, or that you are stopping your collection efforts.

Related Resources

Collecting Assessments: An Operational Guide, 4th Ed. (GAP Report #10). Community Associations Institute, 1996.

   Collecting money is never easy, but this guide will make a self manager's task as efficient as possible. It provides information on a variety of payment systems and suggests which systems are best for different types and sizes of associations. It also provides numerous practical details on how to implement whatever system you decide on. The section on delinquencies provides a good menu of options to pursue before taking legal action. If it does become necessary to take legal action, GAP 5: *Assessment Collection: Legal Remedies* continues the delinquency discussion where this one ends.

Assessment Collection: Legal Remedies (GAP Report #5). Hindman & Sanchez, Community Associations Institute, 2000.

Staying clear of fair debt collection problems shouldn't be unduly burdensome for self managers, particularly when they understand a few basic collection options and the correct approach to legal solutions. GAP 5 discusses the fundamentals of these legal solutions, and should be quite helpful to self managers as they work with their attorneys on collection problems.

Chapter 15

Hiring Practices

Even self-managers find they sometimes need to hire part- or full-time employees. Following a few simple steps will make this process easier for you, and the outcome will be more positive.

Require an Application

Screen applicants carefully. It is much easier *not* to hire the wrong person than to get rid of them after they've become employees. Require each person to complete a comprehensive application that asks for the following information:

- List any criminal convictions.
- Provide extensive employment history, including why he or she left each job.
- Specify what he or she wants to *avoid* in a new job. This prevents you from hiring a person who wants to avoid overtime to fill a job that requires overtime.
- Agree to employment-at-will status.
- Agree to drug testing (if that's your policy).
- Agree to a background check.

Include a statement above the signature line of the application form indicating that the applicant, in signing the form, agrees to abide by your policies, whatever they might be—employment-at-will, drug testing, or background testing. This not only protects you, but it also identifies problem applicants. The applicant who objects to signing such an agreement, or who is preoccupied during the hiring process with preserving his or her right to sue your association, is probably not your best choice.

The Interview

The interview is your opportunity to assess an applicant's honesty and interper-

Employment Application Red Flags

- Multiple changed answers and scratch-outs. Did the applicant need to change standard items like social security numbers, dates of prior jobs, or supervisor's names?
- Key omissions. Did the applicant "forget" to indicate that he or she was convicted of a crime or fired from a job
- Victim-like responses. Did the applicant leave a past job because he or she "disagreed with policy" or had a "personality conflict?"
- Erratic employment history. Did the applicant have unexplained gaps between jobs?

sonal skills. Don't try to sell the job to the applicant during the interview. Focus on finding out if the applicant is a good fit for the job. Save the sales pitch for after you've made your decision. Ask the applicant probing, open-ended questions that will let you know his or her attitudes, reliability, ability to get along with others, and perceptions.

Don't make statements during the interview that the applicant might interpret as or later claim amounted to a guarantee of employment. These might include "We believe in training, not firing," or "Just do a good job and you'll be OK."

Don't make statements or ask questions that might seem discriminatory. Federal law prohibits discrimination in employment based on race, sex, age, national origin, religion, and disability; and state law often prohibits additional types of discrimination, such as national origin and sexual orientation. Therefore, don't ask how old an applicant is, when he or she graduated, what church or synagogue he or she attends, whether she plans on getting married or having children, or whether he or she has ever had health problems or psychiatric treatment. Instead, limit your questions to finding out the applicant's qualifications and ability to perform the job.

Open-Ended Interview Questions

- Do you feel your current job is stressful?
- What do you think of your current supervisor?
- How do you think your current super-visor will respond to my request for a reference?
- What policies of your current employer do you disagree with?
- Do you feel your prior employers treated you fairly?
- Do you currently use illegal drugs?
- What do you think is a satisfactory attendance record?

Drug Testing

Testing applicants for drug use before making an offer of employment is permitted in some jurisdictions. Your drug-screening activities would have to be applied uniformly to every prospective employee in order to be valid, and you'd need a clear, written substance abuse policy that is carefully followed. Your policy should cover what drugs you're testing for, who will be tested and under what conditions, the consequences of testing positive or refusing to take a test, who pays for the drug test, and what the drug-testing procedures are.

Drug testing may be subject to legal restrictions in your area, and you should consult your association attorney for guidance on proper procedures and enforceability of the program.

Check References

Checking references is an important step in the hiring process because it protects you from claims of negligent hiring. For example, if you hired a person without checking references and that person was a known offender, residents could claim that you did not perform due diligence in hiring and thereby failed to protect them.

Have applicants sign a release naming former employers specifically that gives the applicant's consent for you to inquire of their past employment and performance. Some former employers are sensitive to the legal consequences of providing references and they'll only verify basic information like position title and dates of employment. You'll have better luck getting good information if your signed release directly names the former employer.

Consider the source, and remember that different people have different perceptions. Look at all responses from all references equally. Don't allow one comment from one person to sway your decision unduly.

Employment Policies

You should establish and use employment policies. Put them in writing and make them available to all employees. If you want to have an employment-at-will policy (in which you and the employee each have the right to terminate the employment at any time for any reason without having to prove "good cause") then avoid policies that offer "fairness" or "progressive discipline," or assurances that employees will receive warnings before being terminated. Policies like these, or statements like these in em-ployee handbooks, negate the concept of employment-at-will.

Make sure each employee gets a copy of the policies. Have all employees sign a statement indicating that they received the policies and acknowledging that they agree to follow them.

Evaluations

You may be reluctant to appraise the work of your employees realistically because you don't like confrontation or you're concerned that you'll hurt the morale of your staff members. If you're like some supervisors, you'll instead give high marks to mediocre employees. This can cause a problem later if you need to discharge an employee for poor performance.

If you must conduct regular evaluations, use *narrative* evaluations and give constructive criticism and even negative feedback if necessary. Be candid, realistic, and constructive about the employee's performance.

Tips for Checking References

- Prepare your questions ahead of time. Ask the same questions of each reference for each applicant.
- Avoid "in your opinion" questions. Instead ask specific, job-related questions about the applicant's knowledge, skill, ability, and performance.
- Keep detailed records. Note the full name, company, phone number, date, and the name of the applicant for each inquiry you make. Record all answers including "no response" or "did not answer," but don't allow the reference to give you confidential or off-the-record information.
- Verify the information on the application—job title, duties, salary, and dates of employment.
- Don't ask questions that can be considered discriminatory. As with application and interview questions, you can't ask a question if the answer would indicate such details as race, religion, or marital status.

Discipline

Occasionally, you may need to discipline an employee. When you do, put it in writing and have the employee sign a copy. State what will happen if the incident happens again, e.g., the employee will be terminated without further warning. Although you want to avoid progressive discipline as a prerequisite to termination, you do need a record of discipline in an employee's file prior to termination. This protects you from claims of discrimination or other unlawful motive. Also, it's expensive—in time and money—to replace employees, so it's in your best interest to discuss the incident and give employees an opportunity to correct problems before summarily dismissing them.

Standard Employment Policies

- Policy against harassment
- Policy against drug and alcohol abuse
- Rules of conduct, including rules against theft, dishonesty, insubordination, discourtesy, poor attendance, fighting, violence and threats of violence, and the like
- Attendance policy
- Safety and security rules
- Other work rules and procedures

Termination

You can terminate an employee for poor performance, but before you do consider the following questions:

- Was the employee given fair warning of his or her shortcomings?
- Was the warning documented?
- Was the employee given sufficient time to improve?
- Have other employees had similar performance problems? Were they treated consistently?
- Are there any extenuating circumstances that might explain the poor performance?

You can also terminate an employee for misconduct, and again there are a few questions you should ask before you decide:

- Did the misconduct violate a rule that was clear and sufficiently communicated?
- Does the employee admit violating the rule?
- Are there witnesses to the misconduct?
- Is discharge the appropriate penalty?
- Were previous violations of the rule treated consistently?

If you believe an employee should be terminated for misconduct, suspend that person (with or without pay) while you investigate. Avoid a snap decision. It will be much easier to reinstate a suspended employee than to rehire one who's been terminated.

Your investigation should include written statements from the employee and from witnesses. End all written statements with, "I declare under penalty of perjury that the foregoing statement is true and correct." This has the same effect as if the witness gave testimony under oath in court. This may be crucial to avoid or win a wrongful termination lawsuit.

Avoid memos to the file concerning the investigation and its conclusions, since these may have to be surrendered if a lawsuit is filed. Ordinarily, sworn statements from witnesses and the accused employee are the only documentation needed. If you feel you must create additional documentation, put it in a letter to your lawyer so that it will be covered by attorney-client privilege.

Some people are protected by anti-discrimination laws; if you terminate one of them, make sure that other employees with similar performance problems, or who engaged in similar misconduct, are treated similarly. Even though you may have no intent to discriminate, if you terminate an employee in a protected class for misconduct or poor performance but fail to terminate employees outside the protected class for the same misconduct or poor performance, you may be held liable for unlawful discrimination.

Conduct terminations with as much dignity as possible. Notify the employee in private, but have another person present as a witness. You should say as little as possible during the termination meeting. Don't debate or argue, but allow the employee to express his or her feelings. You may also consider giving the employee the opportunity to resign. Have the final paycheck ready at the termination meeting, and collect all keys, computer passwords, and association property at that time.

Maintain confidentiality concerning the termination. Don't announce it to association members or to outside parties. If you're directly asked about the termination, reveal only the facts, and say as little as possible.

If an employee challenges the termination, contact your association attorney immediately.

◆ ◆ ◆ ◆

Hiring doesn't have to be a shot in the dark; your likelihood of finding and keeping good employees will depend on how many of these standard practices you follow.

Sample Documents for Community Association Self-Management

Committees
- Committee Interest Form

Fair Housing
- Sample Procedures: Requesting Reasonable Accommodation for Keeping a Service Animal

Finances
- Sample Delinquency Letter
- Sample Collections Resolution
- Sample Investment Policy 1
- Sample Investment Policy 2

Meetings
- Sample Proxy
- Sample Paragraphs for Minutes
- Sample Minutes for Board of Directors Meeting

Record Keeping
- Sample Community Association Records Retention Schedule

Rules
- Sample Rules for Using the Common Areas
- Sample Request for Design Approval
- Sample Policy Prohibiting Wild Animals as Pets
- Sample Policy Allowing Wild Animals as Pets

Telecommunications
- Sample Letter To Residents Regarding Central Antenna Installation

Committee Interest Form

Date: _____

Name: _____

Address: _____

Phone: _____

E-mail: _____

Committees advise and assist the board in conducting the business of the association. Interested residents of the community are invited to volunteer for committees where they have an interest and can make a contribution to the community. Please check all committees on which you would like to participate.

❑ **Covenants Committee**

Assists the board in regulating external design, appearance, use, and maintenance of the common areas. Issues notices of violations, conducts hearings, and hears appeals. Reviews policies, procedures, rules, and regulations periodically for need and enforceability.

❑ **Communications Committee**

Prepares the association newsletter, promotes community events, maintains a community directory, and conducts orientation for new residents.

❑ **Maintenance Committee**

Preserves and enhances the physical environment of all common areas, solicits information and bids from appropriate maintenance providers, and monitors maintenance contracts for compliance.

❑ **Safety Committee**

Identifies safety hazards, develops programs to promote the safety and security of the community, inspects common areas and equipment, recommends improvements

❑ **Recreation/Social Committee**

Develops social programs according to the needs of the community, and develops programs for all interests and ages.

❑ **Finance Committee**

Reviews the preliminary budget, conducts public hearings on the budget, reviews financial reports, reviews and monitors insurance needs and coverage, monitors financial procedures and transactions.

❑ **Elections Committee**

Nominates candidates for board positions, organizes, prepares for, and conducts association elections.

Please return this form to: _____

Sample Procedures: Requesting Reasonable Accommodation for Keeping a Service Animal

Resident's should submit requests to keep an animal as a reasonable accommodation in writing to the association board of directors.

Qualifying Service Animals
The association may request verification that you are an individual with a disability and/or that the animal has been trained to assist persons with that specific disability. The association will recognize your animal as a "service" or "assistance" animal upon verification. Service animals are exempt from the association's pet policies.

Qualifying Companion Animals
If your animal does not have specific disability-related training, but provides therapeutic or other benefits, the association may recognize the animal as a "companion" animal. The association may request verification that you are in need of therapeutic or other benefit and that the animal provides such benefit. Requests to exempt companion animals from the association's pet policies are considered on a case-by-case basis according to what is legal, reasonable, and fair to all parties involved.

Responsibility for Approved Animals
If your request to exempt your animal from the association pet policies is approved, you will be responsible for the animal's care, and the animal must be kept in a manner consistent with local ordinances. Pet deposits will not be required from owners of approved service, assistance, or companion animals; however, if the animal poses a threat to any resident's health, safety, or enjoyment of the home, your request may be subject to review and revocation.

Sample Delinquency Letter

Our records indicate that your assessment fees are presently in arrears in the amount of $ _____ through ____(date)_____ , including assessments, late charges, and interest which are provided for in the Declaration of Covenants, Conditions, and Restrictions.

We hereby make demand for payment for the above amount that is past due and owing. Unless we receive payment in full or you make satisfactory arrangements for payment immediately, we will file suit against you without further notice to recover this amount. If such action is necessary, you may be found liable for not only the assessment arrearage, but also for interest, late charges, court costs, and attorneys' fees. In addition, we will record a lien against your property with the _____ County Clerk and Recorder; we will also notify your mortgage company of your delinquency, and ask the company to call the balance of your loan due for failure to stay current with your assessment fees as required in your promissory note.

Interest accrues on your balance at _____ percent per month and late fees of $ _____ per month are charged. You are also liable for attorney fees incurred by the association in pursuing this matter under the provisions of the declaration.

Should you fail to dispute this debt or any portion of it, within thirty (30) days of receipt of this letter, we will assumed the debt is correct. You may also request in writing, within thirty (30) days of receipt of this letter, verification of this debt. However, the fact that you may dispute this debt or request verification of it will not delay filing a lawsuit as stated above.

If you advise us in writing to cease contacting you by telephone at your place of employment, we will make no further contacts. If you refuse to pay the debt or you wish us to cease further communication and you so advise us in writing, we won't communicate further with you except to advise you that we intend to invoke specified remedies that we ordinarily invoke and to advise you when we terminate our efforts.

This is an attempt to collect a debt. Any information obtained will be used for that purpose.

We sincerely hope legal action will not be necessary and that you will give this matter your immediate attention. However, should you ignore this letter, we will take legal action.

Very truly yours,

Sample Collections Resolution

The Board of Directors of _____ Association
Adopting a Collection Policy
Adopted _____(date)_____

The following resolution has been adopted by the association pursuant to
_____ law, at a regular meeting of the board of directors.
Whereas the association is charged with certain responsibilities regarding the
care, maintenance, and service of certain portions of the community, and

 Whereas the association must have the financial ability to discharge its
responsibilities, and,

 Whereas the board is required to collect assessments and other charges
from owners, and,

 Whereas the board desires to adopt a uniform, non-discriminating, and systematic procedure to collect assessments and other charges of the association.

 NOW, THEREFORE, BE IT RESOLVED that the ASSOCIATION does
hereby adopt the following procedures and policies for the collection of
assessments and other charges of the association.

 Due Dates. The annual assessment as determined by the association and as
allowed for in the declaration, articles of incorporation, and bylaws shall be
due and payable in _____ installments due on the _____ day of each
month. Assessments or other charges not paid to the association by the
_____ day of the beginning month in which they are due shall be considered past due and delinquent.

 Invoices. The association may, but shall not be required to, invoice an
owner as a condition to an owner's obligation to pay assessments or other
charges of the association. If the association provides an owner with an
invoice for _____ assessments, although invoices are not required, the
invoice should be mailed or sent to the owner between the _____ and
_____ day of the month preceding each due date. Non-receipt of an
invoice shall in no way relieve the owner of the obligation to pay the
amount due by the due date.

 Late Charges Imposed on Delinquent Installments. Assessments shall be past due
and delinquent if not paid as specified above. The association shall impose
a $ _____ late charge on the outstanding or past due balance then due
the association. The late charge shall be a "common expense" for each
owner who fails to pay an installment of the annual assessment by the due
date as specified above.

 The late charge shall be the personal obligation of the owner(s) of the
unit for which such assessment or installment is unpaid. All late charges shall
be due and payable immediately, without notice, in the manner provided by
the declaration (and as set forth above) for payment of assessments.

Interest. The association shall impose interest of _____ % per annum on any unpaid balance. The interest shall be a "common expense" for each owner who fails to pay an installment of the annual assessment by the due date as specified above.

The interest shall be the personal obligation of the owner(s) of the unit for which such assessment or installment is unpaid. All interest shall be due and payable immediately, without notice, in the manner provided by the declaration (and as set forth above) for payment of assessments.

Acceleration of Assessment. Pursuant to _____ ,if an owner's default in paying an installment of any assessment levied against his/her unit continues for (_____) days beyond the due date, the association, at its option, may accelerate the remainder of the _____ assessment and declare them due and payable in full.

Return Check Charges. In addition to any and all charges imposed under the declaration, articles of incorporation, and bylaws, the rules and regulations of the association, or this resolution, a $ _____ fee shall be assessed against an owner in the event any check or other instrument attributable to or payable for the benefit of such owner is not honored by the bank or is returned by the bank for any reason whatsoever, including but not limited to insufficient funds.

This returned check charge shall be a "common expense" for each owner who tenders payment by check or other instrument that is not honored by the bank upon which it is drawn. Such return check charge shall be due and payable immediately, upon demand. Notwithstanding this provision, the association shall be entitled to all additional remedies as may be provided by applicable law.

Returned check charges shall be the obligation of the owner(s) of the unit for which payment was tendered to the association. Return check charges shall become effective on any instrument tendered to the association for payment of sums due under the declaration, articles, bylaws, rules and regulations, or this resolution after _(date)_. If two or more of a unit owner's checks are returned unpaid by the bank within any (fiscal) year, the association may require that all of the unit owner's future payments, for a period of one year, be made by certified check or money order.

Attorney's Fees on Delinquent Accounts. As an additional expense permitted under the declaration, articles, bylaws, and statutes, the association shall be entitled to recover its reasonable attorney's fees and collection costs incurred in the collection of assessments or other charges due the association from a delinquent owner. The reasonable attorney's fees incurred by the association shall be due and payable immediately when incurred, upon demand.

Application for Payments Made to the Association. Payments received from an owner will be credited in the following order:

1. Charges for legal fees, court costs, and other costs of collection

2. All late charges and interest accrued, as applicable

3. All other charges incurred by the association as a result of any violation by an owner, his/her family, employees, agents or licensees, of the declaration, articles of incorporation, bylaws, rules and regulations, or resolutions.

4. The monthly assessment for a unit, including any accelerated or special assessment due, as applicable; payments shall be applied toward the oldest month(s) then owed.

Collection Letters. After an assessment installment or other charge due the association becomes _____ days past due, the association may, but shall not be required to, send a late notice to the unit owner. The association may simultaneously send a copy of the notice to the mortgagee of the unit.

If payment in full is not received within _____ days, the association may, but shall not be required to, send notice to the unit owner that it intends to refer the account to an attorney. The association may simultaneously send a copy of the notice to the mortgagee of the unit.

Use of Certified Mail/Regular Mail. In the event the association shall send a collection or demand letter or notices to a delinquent owner by regular mail, the association may also send, but shall not be required to send, an additional copy of that letter or notice by certified mail.

Liens. The association may file a notice of lien against the property of any delinquent owner in accordance with the terms and provisions of the declaration, articles of incorporation, and bylaws. A copy of the notice of lien shall be mailed to the owner and to the mortgage lender with a request that the lender send a letter to the delinquent owner advising the owner of the lender's option to accelerate the mortgage debt.

Referring Delinquent Accounts to Attorneys. The association may, but shall not be required to, refer delinquent accounts to an attorney for collection. Upon referral to the attorney, the attorney shall take all appropriate action to collect the accounts referred.

Referring Delinquent Accounts to Collection Agencies. The association may, but shall not be required to, refer delinquent accounts to one or more collection agencies for collection. Upon referral to a collection agency, the agency shall take all appropriate action to collect the accounts referred.

The association may grant a waiver of any provision herein upon petition in writing by an owner showing a personal hardship. Such relief granted an owner shall be appropriately documented in the files with the name of the person or persons representing the association granting the relief and the conditions of the relief. In addition, the association is hereby authorized to extend the time for the filing of lawsuits and liens, or to otherwise modify the procedures contained herein, as the association shall determine appropriate under the circumstances.

Notification to Owners. The association shall cause all owners to be notified of this resolution and the late charges, returned check charge, and attorney's fees to be imposed after the effective date of those provisions of this resolution. All other policies and procedures set forth in this resolution shall be effective immediately.

Ongoing Evaluation. Nothing in this resolution shall require the association to take specific actions other than to notify homeowners of the adoption of these policies and procedures. The association has the option and right to continue to evaluate each delinquency on a case-by-case basis.

IN WITNESS WHEREOF, the undersigned have executed this resolution the _____ day of _____ , in the year _____

Sample Investment Policy 1

BE IT RESOLVED that the replacement reserves shall be invested in such amounts as may be authorized by the board of directors in accord with the following policy.

A. No funds shall be deposited or invested except in authorized investments. Authorized investments are those that are in accordance with the state Condominium Act and with the declaration and bylaws of this association and that are obligations of, or fully guaranteed by, the U.S. government.

B. All accounts, instruments, and other documentation of such investments shall be subject to the approval of, and may from time to time be amended by, the board of directors as appropriate, and they shall be reviewed at least annually.

C. Investments shall be guided by the following goals, listed in decreasing order of importance:

1. Safety of principal. The long-term goal is safety of the replacement reserves.

2. Liquidity and accessibility. Funds should be readily available for projected or unexpected expenditures.

3. Minimal costs. Investment costs (redemption fees, commissions, and other transaction costs) should be minimized.

4. Professional management. Funds should be invested with professional managers who have good reputations and sound credentials.

5. Return. Funds should be invested to seek the highest level of return that is consistent with preservation of the purchasing power of the principle and accumulated interest.

Sample Investment Policy 2

Association directors have a fiduciary duty to prudently manage reserve assets. Accordingly, the directors have set forth an investment policy to pursue association objectives and goals. The policy is based on historical bond rates, money market instruments, and inflation. The directors expect that over time the strategy will produce results consistent with history and meet the reserve fund's goals.

Goals and Objectives. The association's capital replacement reserve assets shall be invested to achieve the following objectives.

1. Promote and ensure the preservation of the reserve fund's principal.

2. Structure maturities to ensure availability of assets.

3. Mitigate the effects of interest rate volatility upon reserve assets.

4. Achieve long-term investment performance that exceeds inflation by 1 to 3 percent on a net after-tax basis.

Investment Strategy. Select securities that mature in one to five years. Structure them so that an equal number mature each year. Consistently purchase securities at the long end of the maturity range with new or matured funds.

Reserve assets will benefit from long-term rates, which are often higher than short-term rates, while maintaining ready availability of funds and cash flow.

The association may veer from this strategy when reserving a portion for a specific expense. Use the most recent reserve study to match the effective maturities to the dates of the expenses. *Effective maturity* may be sooner than *stated maturity.*

Selection Criteria. Securities will be selected with an emphasis on these characteristics: preservation of capital; quality; effective maturity; and net after-tax return.

Cash Equivalents. Money market funds of a bank or major brokerage firm; bank certificates of deposit; AAA-rated municipal or U.S. treasury securities with maturities of one year or less.

Fixed Income. Utilize taxable income securities for association income that is taxable in the lower brackets. Invest in tax-exempt securities above that level if the after-tax return is favorable. The taxable portion shall consist of U.S. treasury securities and insured bank certificates of deposit.

Tax-exempt securities will be rated in the AAA-quality level by at least one major credit rating agency at the time of purchase or be of equivalent quality if non-rated.

An issue-by-issue review will be conducted for each security that has its credit rating lowered after purchase and for each security presently in the portfolio that falls below these criteria. A decision will be made to either hold and monitor or liquidate.

Beyond quality considerations, selection criteria will emphasize securities' maturities before yields. This emphasis is recognized as essential to the governing investment strategy.

Review and Control. The directors will meet at least quarterly. Policy considerations concerning changes of investment strategy or security selection criteria will also require a meeting to obtain a consensus.

The performance review will be compared to the goals and objectives of the reserve fund. The directors will recognize the price volatility of fixed-income investments and not the strategy to hold such securities to their fixed value at maturity.

The board will deliver monthly reserve statements to the manager. These statements will provide detailed accounting of current values, income, and transactions. Additional, customized reports will be available on request.

Sample Proxy

I, the undersigned, being a bona fide member in good standing of the
_____ association, Inc., and as such entitled to
cast one (1) vote at the annual meeting of said association, do hereby appoint
_____ of _____
        [Printed name]   [Address]
as my proxy to attend said meeting with full power to vote for me in my
name, place, and stead in the same manner and to the same extent and with
the same effect that I might were I personally present.

_____

Signature   Date

Please print your name, address, and phone number here:

_____
_____
_____
_____

Accepted this _____ day of _____.

_____

Secretary, ABC Homeowners Association, Inc.

Note: *This is a sample; your association attorney may have more appropriate samples for
your situation. Since improper proxy forms can invalidate an election or meeting, you should
ask an attorney to review whatever proxy form you wish to use.*

Sample Language: Meeting Minutes

Special Board Meeting. A special meeting of the board of directors was held at the association clubhouse, Houston, Texas, on October 21, 2002, at 10:45 A.M., pursuant to the call of the president.

Purpose of Special Board Meeting. The president stated that the purpose of the special board meeting was to accept with regret the resignation of the manager and to select a successor in a timely and orderly manner.

Opening Paragraph to Continue an Adjourned Meeting. An adjourned meeting of the board of directors of the Pinewood Association was held at the association clubhouse, Houston, Texas, on February 19, 2002, at 6:30 P.M., pursuant to an adjournment of a meeting held on January 30, 2002, at the same time and place.

Dispensing With the Reading of the Minutes. Copies of the minutes of the meeting of the board of directors held on February 19, 2002, having been mailed to each director six (6) days prior to the meeting, the directors present agree to dispense with the reading of the minutes, and approved and adopted them as they appeared in the copies received by them.

Chairman. Director A acted as chairman of the meeting and Mrs. C as secretary of the meeting.

Quorum. The directors present at the meeting were Mr. A, Mrs. C, Mr. F, Mrs. B, and Mrs. D, constituting a quorum of the authorized number of the directors of the association.

Lack of a Quorum. A regular meeting of the board of directors of the Pinewood Association was scheduled for Monday, October 21, 2002, at the association clubhouse, Houston, Texas, at 10:45 A.M. The following directors were present at the place specified: Mr. A, and Mrs. B. No quorum being present, the meeting was duly adjourned, as provided for in the bylaws of the association, to October 31, 2002, at the association clubhouse, Houston, Texas, at 6:30 P.M.

Close a Meeting. There being no further business before the meeting, on motion made, seconded, and carried, the meeting was adjourned at 9:30 P.M.

The Absence of a Meeting. In the absence of a meeting, but as approved by all directors as witnessed by their initials and signatures below, the following actions were taken in accordance with Article 4, Section 2 of the bylaws of the Pinewood Association. As of this date, the directors of the association are: Mr. A, Mrs. B, Mrs. C, Mrs. D, and Mr. F. The undersigned further certify that they constitute all of the directors of the association entitled to vote on the foregoing resolutions and that the adoption of such resolutions by unanimous written consent of the directors is authorized by the bylaws of the association.

Sample Minutes: Board of Directors Meeting

Minutes of the ABC Community Association
Board of Directors Meeting
February 19, 2002

Date and Time
Pursuant to Article _____, Section _____of the association bylaws, a regular meeting of the board of directors was held on February 19, 2002, at 6:30 P.M. at the office of the association president, Mr. A.

Officers Present
The president, Mr. A, opened the meeting at 6:30 P.M. The secretary, Mrs. P, was present to record the meeting.

Quorum
The following directors were present: Mrs. A, Mrs. B, Mrs. C, and Mr. F.

Minutes
The minutes of the January 20, 2002, meeting were distributed to all directors and committee chairpersons one week before the meeting. The following corrections were made:

Page 1, Paragraph 3: change "lien" to "line"

Page 7, Paragraph 4: substitute "review" for "report"

There being no other corrections or additions, a motion was made by Mr. B to accept the minutes as corrected. The motion was seconded by Mr. F. and approved unanimously.

Finance Report
The treasurer asked if there were any questions relating to the annual audit that had been distributed with the agenda. He noted that Resolution 8 provided that copies be made available to all members who submitted a written request for the audit.

Old Business
Parking: A motion was made by Mrs. B and seconded by Mr. F to adopt the proposed parking policy resolution (attached). The motion was approved unanimously.

Playground equipment: A motion was made by Mr. F and seconded by Mrs. C to table discussion of new equipment until all directors were present. The motion was approved unanimously.

New Business

CAI Meeting: A motion was made by Mrs. C and seconded by Mrs. B that the directors attending the conference be reimbursed for the cost of parking at the airport, pursuant to the existing policy of the board on reimbursement for educational events. The motion was approved. Mr. F voted against the motion.

Adjourn

There being no other business, a motion was made, seconded, and unanimously approved to adjourn the meeting at 9:00 P.M.

_____   _____

Mrs. P, Secretary   Mr. A, President

_____   _____

Date   Date

Sample Community Association Records
Retention Schedule

File Name	Current File	Storage
Annual Reports	2 years	Permanently
Articles of Incorporation	Permanently	
As-Built Specification Plans	Permanently	
Assessment Information	1 year	7 years
Assessment Status	1 year	7 years
Bank Reconciliation	1 year	1 year
Budget	1 year	Permanently
Cancelled Checks and Bank Statements	1 year	7 years
Cash Disbursements Journal	1 year	Permanently
Cash Receipts Journal	1 year	Permanently
Certificates of Insurance	1 year	7 years
Committee Reports	1 year	3 years
Contracts	1 year	7 years
Correspondence: General Matters	1 year	3 years
Correspondence: Legal and Contract	1 year	Permanently
Declaration	Permanently	
Deeds	Permanently	
Duplicate Deposit Tickets	1 year	1 year
Employee Applications	1 year	1 year
Employee Files	1 year	7 years
Federal Income Tax Returns	3 Years	Permanently
Monthly Financial Statements	1 year	7 years
General Ledgers	1 year	Permanently
General Journals	1 year	Permanently
State and Federal Identification Numbers	Permanently	
Insurance Policies	1 year	7 years
Open Insurance Claims	Until Settled	
Settled Insurance Claims	1 year	7 years
Investment Statements & Closed Passbooks	1 year	7 years
Supply Invoices	1 year	7 years
Unexpired Leases		Until Expired

File Name	Current File	Storage
Expired Leases	7 years	
Open Legal Files	Until Closed	
Closed Legal Files	1 year	Permanently
Mailing Lists	1 year	
Management Notices	1 year	3 years
Board Meeting Minutes	1 year	Permanently
Newsletters	1 year	3 years
Payroll Records	1 year	7 years
Plat of Survey	Permanently	
Proposals	1 year	7 years
Purchase Orders	1 year	1 year
Real Estate Taxes	1 year	7 years
Right of First Refusal Letters	1 year	Permanently
Rules and Regulations	Permanently	
State Income Tax Returns	3 years	Permanently
State and Federal Unemployment Taxes	3 years	Permanently
Unexpired Warranties		Until Expired
Expired Warranties	7 years	
State and Federal Withholding Taxes	3 years	Permanently

Sample Rules for Using the Common Areas

The common lands are a great natural asset for association residents. These lands were permanently set aside to maintain a natural buffer between residential and commercial areas, and they were established to benefit current and future residents of the community. They provide an educational area for those interested in plants and wildlife.

The preservation of these lands depends primarily on the cooperation of association residents. Preservation is only partially assured through the official activities of the association.

These lands are owned by the association and maintained with dues paid to the association.

The association is responsible for developing natural and created features on the common lands. The association is also responsible for hiring professionals to develop landscape plans and to design common-land facilities.

The association urges residents to make suggestions for the development of the common lands; to donate, through the maintenance committee, plants or facilities for the common lands; and to help maintain the lands by removing litter or rubbish from the common lands.

Our investment in the common land can be enhanced and maintenance costs kept at a reasonable level if certain rules are followed.

Therefore, the association has set the following rules for common area use:

- Do not plant, cultivate, or harvest natural resources on the common lands.
- Do not place personal structures or store equipment on the common land.
- Do not discard refuse on common lands.
- Motor-driven vehicles are not permitted on walkways or common lands.
- Open fires on the common land are not permitted except where facilities are provided.
- Glass or metal containers other than nursing bottles are not permitted in the tot lots.
- Bicycles are not permitted on the common land except for designated bike paths.
- Loud and boisterous activity on the common land after dark is not permitted.

Sample Request for Design Approval

Owner Name: _____

Date: _____

Property Address: _____

Mailing Address (if different): _____

Work Phone: _____

Home Phone: _____

E-Mail: _____

Please submit your request for design approval in writing. Your request should include:

1. A description of the change or addition

2. A copy of your property plat showing:
    a. the exact location of the proposed change or addition
    b. the distance to your property lines from the proposed change
    c. the dimensions of your property
    d. the dimensions of relevant surrounding features

3. A reasonably accurate rendering showing:
    a. style
    b. dimensions
    c. materials
    d. colors
    e. construction schedule

Requests for repainting must include a color sample.

Incomplete requests will be deferred until all information is received. Requests may also be deferred if the committee requires additional information for any reason.

Important Considerations:
1. Requests from owners with delinquent assessment accounts will be denied on the basis of the account delinquency. Once the assessment account is brought current, the design review committee will review and act on the request.
2. The owner understands and agrees that no work in this request shall commence until written approval by the design review committee is received.
3. Once approved, construction must be completed within the approved

construction time and must be done in a way that does not unreasonably interfere with neighboring properties.

4. Applicant has responsibility to remove all construction debris in a timely manner.

5. Construction must meet all zoning, building codes, and laws of the county. For further information regarding zoning, call _____ and for construction specifications (building permits) call _____ . Further, nothing herein contained shall be construed as a waiver or modification of any such code or law.

6. Where applicable, utility easements are to be marked before construction is started. For information on who to contact, call _____ . You will be fined if utility lines or conduits are damaged.

7. Misrepresentation of any items in this request, either oral or written, may void any approval by this committee.

I have read the design review committee guidelines. This proposed change or addition meets the requirements and standards specific in these guidelines.

Owner signature _____

Date _____

Sample Policy: Prohibiting Wild Animals as Pets

Our community association subscribes to the policy of the American Association of Zoos and Aquariums with regard to harboring wild animals as pets: "In view of the hazards both to animals and to man, and due to the specialized expertise required to properly care for captive wildlife, the American Association of Zoos and Aquariums recommends that wild animals not be kept as pets, and further, that the general public keep only domestic animals as pets."

Therefore, our community association specifically prohibits harboring wild animals other than domestic animals as defined by the Humane Society of the United States.

Residents who fail to comply with the terms of this policy will be reported to local animal-control authorities.

Sample Policy: Allowing Wild Animals as Pets

Our community association subscribes to the policy of the American Association of Zoos and Aquariums with regard to harboring wild animals as pets: "In view of the hazards both to animals and to man, and due to the specialized expertise required to properly care for captive wildlife, the American Association of Zoos and Aquariums recommends that wild animals not be kept as pets, and further, that the general public keep only domestic animals as pets."

While the association does not endorse harboring wild animals as pets, neither does it prohibit the practice. However, the association does require that residents who chose to harbor wild animals as pets comply with all local, state, and federal regulations regarding their keeping. Residents are required to provide the association with documentation indicating that they are in compliance.

Resident who choose to harbor wild animals as pets must maintain liability insurance of not less than $1 million in coverage. Proof of coverage must be provided to the association.

Residents who fail to comply with applicable laws regarding harboring wild animals as pets or with the terms of this policy will be reported to local animal-control authorities.

Sample Letter To Residents: Installing a Central Antenna

Dear Resident:

The association has recently decided to install a central antenna to make some types of service available to all residents. If you'd like to receive these services, please call the association or your preferred telecommunications provider.

Because of the addition of this central antenna, you may **not** install individual antennas, **if**:

- The central antenna offers the services you want;
- The central antenna allows you to use the provider you want;
- The reception from the central antenna is as good as you could get from an individual antenna;
- Your cost for the central antenna isn't *more than* the installation, maintenance, and use of an individual antenna; and
- Using the central antenna doesn't cause you to wait for video programming.

We selected the central antenna service based on information collected from residents. However, if you want to receive another service from another provider, you may. The association will work with you to add the service to the central antenna or allow you to install your individual antenna as quickly as possible.

If you install an individual antenna after receiving this letter, but before we install the central antenna, we will ask you to remove it at our expense and we will reimburse you for value of the antenna. If this happens, we'll notify you ahead of time.

Please call _____ if you have questions about the central antenna.

Sincerely,

COMMUNITY
ASSOCIATIONS
INSTITUTE

About Community Associations Institute (CAI)

Community Associations Institute (CAI) is a national, nonprofit 501(c)(6) association created in 1973 to provide education and resources to America's 231,000 residential condominiums, cooperatives, and homeowner associations, and related professionals and service providers. The Institute is dedicated to fostering vibrant, responsive, competent community associations that promote harmony, community, and responsible leadership.

As a multidisciplinary alliance, CAI serves all stakeholders in community associations. CAI members include condominium and homeowner associations, cooperatives, and association-governed planned communities of all sizes and architectural types; individual homeowners; community association managers and management firms; public officials; and lawyers, accountants, engineers, reserve specialists, builder/developers, and other providers of professional services and products for community associations. CAI has nearly 17,000 members in its chapters throughout the U.S. and in several foreign countries. The national office is in Alexandria, Virginia.

How does CAI serve its members?

- CAI advances excellence through seminars, workshops, conferences, and education programs, some of which lead to professional designations.

- CAI publishes the largest collection of resources available on community associations, including books, guides, *Common Ground* magazine, and specialized newsletters on community association finance, law, and management.

- CAI advocates community association interests before legislatures, regulatory bodies, and the courts.

- CAI conducts research and acts as a clearinghouse of information on innovations and best practices in community association creation and management.

- CAI provides networking and referral opportunities through both the national office and local CAI chapters, CAI-sponsored insurance programs for directors and officers, a 401(k) retirement plan, and discounts on products and services.

How can I get more information on CAI or on community associations?

For membership or other information, call the national office at (703) 548-8600 (M-F, 9-5:30 ET) or visit CAI's Web site at www.caionline.org.